THE GREAT BELOW

A JOURNEY INTO LOSS

Maddy Paxman

THE GREAT BELOW
A JOURNEY INTO LOSS

Published by
Garnet Publishing Limited
8 Southern Court
South Street
Reading
RG1 4QS
UK

www.garnetpublishing.co.uk
www.twitter.com/Garnetpub
www.facebook.com/Garnetpub
blog.garnetpublishing.co.uk

Copyright © Maddy Paxman, 2014

First Edition

ISBN: 9781859643761

British Library Cataloguing-in-Publication Data
A catalogue record for this book is available from the British Library

Typeset by Samantha Barden
Jacket design by Arash Hejazi
Cover images Empty white interior of a vintage room without
ceiling from grey grunge stone wall and old wood floor © cluckva,
courtesy of Shutterstock.com and photo from the
author's private collection
Author photograph © Caroline Penn

Printed and bound in Lebanon by International Press:
interpress@int-press.com

'*From the Great Above she opened her ear to the Great Below.*'
From *The Descent of Inanna*, translated from the Sumerian
by Diane Wolkstein and Samuel Noah Kramer.

'*He says the best way out is always through.*
And I agree to that, or in so far
As that I can see no way out but through . . .'
Robert Frost, 'A Servant to Servants'.

*For Michael, who I wish had been able to read this,
and for Ruairi, who I hope one day will.*

PREFACE

My husband, the poet Michael Donaghy, died on Thursday 16 September 2004, having suffered a brain haemorrhage the previous weekend. He was fifty and I was four years younger. It was one of those bright, crisp autumn days in a whole week of beautiful days. I stood at his feet and held on to his dear familiar toes, as if still trying to ground him, while the nurse removed the breathing tube. In the process she accidentally scratched his throat, which made him utter a choking cough; it was the first time since he became unconscious on Sunday that I had heard the sound of his voice and the last time I ever would. 'Sorry, Michael, so sorry!' she said.

For a moment, it wasn't clear to me what had happened; I asked: 'Has he gone?' and she said yes. He quickly began to turn blue, as I had been warned. I laid my head on his chest where I could hear his heart still beating strongly; it continued to do so for what seemed ages and I thought how much Michael had worried about his heart and yet here it was, almost outliving him with its sturdy rhythm. 'Silly bugger', I told him quietly. But then the sound came to an end and he was still. His skin colour began to return to pink. My sister was weeping quietly but I felt calm, almost euphoric.

We had been given a quiet curtained-off space in an empty ward for the end game. The ward sister, whose shift had officially ended at lunchtime, had stayed on with us into the evening to be with us through the death, like a midwife for the end of life.

(In the old days it was the same women who guided people into life and out of it: both assisting at births and laying out bodies for burial.) This, on a busy neurosurgery ward where many patients do not survive, was the most generous of acts; we felt held, contained, but never hurried.

In a version of an age-old ritual I had helped to wash Michael's body in preparation; they let me cut his toenails and I noticed that, ironically, the terrible athlete's foot which had recently been giving him such trouble had completely cleared up. The nurse gave him a shave, a job she said she liked, but nothing could be done about his hair which was still matted with blood from the operation that had cut open his skull, and was now stiff with sweat. Finally we dressed him in a fresh hospital gown; printed in yellow and red with the words 'For hospital use only', it reminded me of a hamburger wrapping.

I would have liked to have candles or anointing oils but Health and Safety forbade them. So instead we had a little interlude of poetry and song to send him on his way. I recited 'The Present', one of his poems, from memory, getting the last line slightly wrong. Then I sang a song that I used to sing to him when we were young and first in love: 'To Althea from Prison' with words by Sir Walter Raleigh set to an Irish melody, a song about how the spirit can be free even when the body is in chains. For good measure I ended with a funny song Michael had made up for our eight-year-old son, Ruairi, which begins 'You've got to keep a chicken on your head . . .'

Outside the light was fading and inside the ward lights were dimmed, so the room had a grey peacefulness about it as we said goodbye. I've thought a lot about those final moments: how we made the choice which modern medicine has created for us, whether to continue to keep someone artificially alive or let them go. In effect, we finished him off like a wounded animal. What an awesome and awful task to have to perform as a doctor or nurse, no matter how used to death you have become.

The final checks – pulse, temperature, a torch flashed in the eyes to see if the pupils are at all reactive – still no contraction, clearly brain-dead. And then we unplug him.

At the very moment of his dying a close friend of his called the hospital; she had heard him call out her name quite loudly inside her head. Another friend reported feeling a sudden sense of peace, the fretful anxiety of the past few days lifting like a cloud. One of our son's teachers later told me that she had felt suddenly breathless at that particular moment, and had a sense that it might all be over. Several of Michael's friends told me of dreams they had that night; one dreamed that she and he were lying flat on the ground in New York, making 'snow angels' by flapping their arms to make the imprint of wings. He told her: 'I used to worry a lot about this, but it's really fine.'

Afterwards he lay on the bed, seeming no more dead or alive really than he had been moments before, than he had been for four days. I wondered how I would possibly be able to leave, to take the last sight of this man I had loved for twenty-one years, who had been my soul-mate, best friend, co-parent, latterly husband, and also my burden. But as I sat on, my thoughts turned to Ruairi who was with a close friend, and it was like hearing a call from life to come, pay attention. 'Let the dead bury their dead.' I paused at the curtain, looked back once, left.

CHAPTER 1

The haemorrhage happened on Sunday morning, 12 September 2004, although it had probably been developing for a few weeks previously, during which Michael had had a couple of strange fainting spells. We had spent the past week in Spain, where he was teaching a residential poetry course, and I was trying, not with great success, to hijack it into a family holiday; combining work and leisure is never a wise gambit but it was often the only way I could persuade Michael to go away.

The course was held in a beautiful villa in a small town perched above a valley full of lemon and almond trees, up in the mountains inland from Alicante. Things got off to a bad start when I realised on the plane that I'd forgotten my driving licence and we would be unable to hire the car we'd booked; we had instead to take a long, winding minibus trip up to the village, which made both Michael and Ruairi travel-sick. Thereafter we were effectively stranded there for the week in 40-degree heat; I lay in the shade reading and Ruairi spent the day jumping in and out of the freezing 'infinity edge' pool, or looking for small lizards in the cracks of the stone walls. One night I dreamed that while roller skating he had rolled off the side into the pool, and I could see him lying there at the bottom with his eyes open. I knew I needed to save him, but I too had roller skates on and was afraid if I jumped in I might sink. Later, seeing Michael unconscious in hospital would remind me of this dream, as though it had been a premonition.

Michael was working practically all the time; the programme was very full, including evening sessions, and even when off-duty on residential courses you have to socialise with the students. He had been feeling very unwell – sick and groggy – ever since our arrival and one morning almost passed out while teaching. We put it down to intolerance of the heat; despite growing up in stifling New York summers, he had suffered severe heat-stroke on a trip to Mexico City a few years before. Our hosts suggested he see a doctor, but he had very recently been to see our GP in England, and was I think slightly anxious about the language barrier. Besides, as he was someone who never felt in the peak of health, with a constant stream of amorphous and shifting symptoms, it was hard to take all of this very seriously.

We spent hardly any time together that week, and when we did there was an undercurrent of griping anger and frustration. Despite the kind attentiveness of our hosts, I was bored and lonely; he was sick and stressed. It's strange and sad to think now that in our last week together we were so far apart, in the way that only a warring couple can be. I remember just one evening when, alone together on the terrace after dinner, our old connection seemed to flower and we held hands and looked out in wonder at the thousands of stars hanging over the dark valley. In the distance you could hear sounds of fireworks from another village – a wedding or fiesta – but we stood there together in the quiet of suspended time. In some ways I think of this as our last moment of peace, a brief taste of eternity.

As we left the villa on our last day I picked a very ripe fig from the tree behind the house – one of only two left on the tree. It had the most astonishingly intense flavour and sweetness, and suddenly I understood all those fairy-tales and myths where you eat the forbidden fruit and are forever enchanted. Something in me demanded more, immediately! There was, however, only one more fruit and it was hanging way out over the ravine where I would probably kill myself trying to pick it. I left with the taste of a new experience, a new sensuality, in my mouth that seemed almost a glimpse into another way of interacting with the world.

The irritable mood between us persisted through the journey home and the business of unpacking and doing laundry, the burden of which always seemed to fall on me. The morning after we got back Michael was due to play an Irish music gig with an old friend, and though he woke up feeling worse than ever he was determined not to let them down. I suggested he go back to bed for a while and that I would call him when it was time to leave. I was hanging out the washing in the back garden when he yelled down in panic through the open bedroom window that he couldn't move his left arm and leg. My first reaction was 'What NOW?' and I'm not proud of the way I dealt with him that morning – brusque and irritated when he was obviously quite terrified. Of course, had I known what was coming I hope I would have found it in me to be kinder.

To be fair to myself I had lived for years with what I think of as poet's hypochondria. Many poets are rather sickly creatures, prone to severe health anxieties and often taking to their beds – one I know even sees the doctor regularly for his hypochondriasis. A poetic explanation might be that the practice of their art keeps them too close to the higher realms for them to feel truly comfortable on earth. Then again, maybe they just spend too much time navel-gazing, being possibly the most self-absorbed of all artists. An old girlfriend of Michael's warned me that the first thing he said every morning was 'Ouch!' and it's true that something always hurt: a toe, an eyebrow, an internal organ. I look at it now as his body's attempt to ground him on earth – saying 'Hey! Here I am!' He was capable of developing the most astonishing symptoms under emotional pressure, once sprouting a large egg-shaped lump on his back after we had had a row. Yet despite all this I hardly ever saw him take a day off work, let alone miss a reading. He once travelled to Glasgow to give a performance with a fever of 104 degrees and a swollen spleen that the doctor thought might indicate hepatitis. The show must go on.

Only a few months earlier he had set off on a reading tour of the US with what turned out to be a seriously inflamed gall bladder. He ended up in hospital having an emergency procedure to unblock the bile duct, but got up the next day to give the reading he was booked to do. One night in New York – I had tagged us along on the early part of this trip as well – I sat up keeping him company while he endured the excruciating pain in his guts brought on by an unwise glass of wine and it suddenly dawned on me that my husband, for all his anxiety and complaining, was incredibly stoic when it came to pain.

All this made it impossible to know when he was really ill and when it was just hypochondria as usual. Over the past couple of years there had been a succession of trips to A&E with suspected heart attacks, which are a common cause of anxiety in middle-aged men, especially if, like Michael, their father had died that way. He was finally diagnosed with a slightly unusual heart rhythm – 'right bundle branch block' – which was not life-threatening, but the slightest strange sensation in his chest would trigger a spiralling panic reaction; I often caught him anxiously holding a hand to his chest or surreptitiously taking his pulse. I found it very hard to take any of his symptoms seriously, even when he was strapped up to monitors in a hospital bed; I just felt cross and put-upon. After a couple of these false alarms I even stopped going with him to the hospital, just packing him off in the ambulance alone.

I'm not sure why I always felt so angry when he was ill; perhaps it made him seem even more dependent on me than usual. I have had my share of illness and when I am sick I want plenty of attention and nurturing, which Michael was largely incapable of giving. He was broadly sympathetic, but assumed you just wanted to be left alone to sleep, whereas I wanted meals in bed, company, above all someone to take over my role as chief cook and bottle-washer. When I was little, there were rewards for being ill and I exploited this discovery frequently; it was practically the only time when I felt I got my mother's full attention. I would be tucked up in her big bed and assiduously mothered with bowls of bread in warm milk, read to or allowed to watch TV, treated with kindness and sympathy; whereas any kind of emotional difficulty on my part usually sparked a cold fury and withdrawal. Perhaps I felt that by being ill Michael was stealing my thunder, my rightful place in the sickbed?

That Sunday morning, the beginning of the end, I think I was both furious and frankly terrified. Here was I, struggling to keep things together and look after Ruairi, and Michael was starting yet another round of weird dramatic symptoms. He was correspondingly enraged with me for not taking him seriously and being so unsympathetic. Wearily I called out the ambulance, which arrived in record time. The paramedics didn't appear unduly concerned about the fact that he was paralysed all down his left side; they refused to be drawn on causes but seemed to regard it as a temporary condition which would wear off. They carried him downstairs, loaded him into the ambulance and drove him to the hospital, not even turning on the blue light. I decided to finish hanging out the last load of washing before following on in the car with Ruairi; I can see now that I was acting pretty strangely in the circumstances.

When things go badly in hospitals they tend to go wrong in small increments; often no one thing is the tipping point into catastrophe but little by little the delays and misjudgements pile up. My experience of hospitals, particularly this one, over the years is that you arrive in Accident and Emergency thinking with relief, 'Now I'm safe; I'll be looked after.' But then you are left languishing in a corridor or cubicle or waiting-room in what appears to be a hospital empty of medical staff: no information, no treatment, no one around to ask. If there are medical personnel in view they are always busy tapping into computers, or talking to each other and ignoring you. However serious or minor your problem, it seems the real action is always happening elsewhere and you must wait your turn. Although I know the Health Service is underfunded and over-stretched, I can't help feeling this is fundamentally a problem of management: a misunderstanding of the needs of anxious patients for reassurance and to be kept in the picture.

You would think that a fifty-year-old man brought in by ambulance and paralysed down one side of his body would be treated as a serious emergency, but it was at least two hours before we were seen by the first doctor. Many things were working against us that day. It was a Sunday morning in September, when all the new young doctors were starting their jobs – sweet and eager, they all looked about fifteen. There was, I later learned, a surge of 'high priority' cases who came in at the same time as Michael – though I would have thought he merited the same designation. There was also, amazingly, no consultant on duty, just one on call by telephone, which I still find extraordinary – allowing a large hospital emergency depart-ment, at the busiest time, to be run by less experienced and even junior doctors. Additionally, there are no radiographers in hospitals at weekends, owing to a national shortage: they too are on call and can be paged to come in, but of course that takes time (and costs money, no doubt). All in all we could hardly have chosen a worse moment.

This particular hospital, which is our local one, has always shown reluctance to use diagnostic technology. Years ago I was sent home bleeding internally from an ectopic pregnancy, because the single ultrasound scanner was being used on another ward; I almost died. On the other end of the scale, when I broke a toe I was lucky to be seen by an agency nurse who ordered an immediate X-ray. The doctor I saw afterwards told me they didn't usually bother with this procedure, since there was nothing that could be done anyway. I pointed out to her that it made quite a difference to know whether I would be incapacitated for six weeks if it were broken, or a matter of days if it were only a sprain.

The atmosphere in the A&E was far from comforting. This was a large, busy inner-city hospital still coping with the fallout from Saturday night. After a few basic checks by a nurse we were abandoned in a grim curtained cubicle, from which I had to make constant forays through two locked doors: to the hospital shop for things to keep Ruairi entertained; and to make mobile phone calls outside the front entrance. Michael was unable to get up or even sit up, so when he needed to pee I had to ask for a bottle and hold it steady for him while he leant against me for support. (I remembered doing something similar once early in our relationship, when he was too drunk to get up the stairs after a party.) A violent patient locked in a room next to our cubicle and guarded by police regularly hammered on the door howling: 'Let me out – I'm a DOCTOR!!!' The ladies toilet was covered with blood and no one came to clean it all day despite my reporting it several times.

The angry tension between Michael and me continued, although I tried my best to override it. I knew I wasn't behaving well but I think now that we were both acting out of fear: what if he'd had a stroke and was going to be disabled long-term? He certainly would not be a patient patient, and my life – and Ruairi's – would be over. Eventually a young woman doctor came and took a medical history, then carried out a series of reaction tests that might indicate a stroke; she said it was probably a Transient Ischaemic Attack (a small stroke) and would resolve over the next day or so. She left saying she would pass him on to the 'medical team'. You get caught up in this mysterious language in hospital – wasn't she 'medical'? I later learned that in her notes she had described Michael's left-side paralysis as 'weakness' and wrongly stated the cause of his mother's death as a heart attack.

As yet nobody seemed to be taking this very seriously, so consequently neither did I. At this point I was even thinking I might still make it to my book group that evening, leaving Michael safe in hospital. Accordingly I went to the shop again to buy him some reading matter he might like; I chose a science magazine with an article about how we are all made of stardust. Guilt comes with the territory of grief because when someone has died there is no longer a chance to put things right or say sorry. I regret now not being a better advocate, not making more of a fuss to get him properly diagnosed. But deep down I don't believe that it would have made a difference to the outcome – his time was well and truly up. I sometimes think that our arrival in the A&E on that particularly chaotic day was essentially to speed him on the journey, because even if it's remotely possible that he could have been kept alive by prompter treatment, it might well have been to a life worse than death.

We waited another two hours in the cubicle, during which time Michael repeatedly struggled and failed to move his left leg. If I lifted it up into a bent position for him he could, with tremendous sweating effort, thrust it straight. Ruairi became understandably fractious and bored; I was still trying to find someone to come and pick him up, but everyone I rang was out or otherwise occupied. The next doctor we saw, also young and female, asked the same questions about medical history and ran the same series of reaction tests; after four hours Michael was no better or worse, but no one seemed to know exactly what had happened. It made me long for the American system of over-investigating everything for fear of legislation, or at any rate for the wonderful fictitious urgency of doctors in TV hospital dramas like *ER*.

This second young doctor clearly fell in love with us as a family, or at least with the delightful man and the adorable child, who never failed to pull out the charm when it was called for, no matter how grim they were feeling. Once when Michael had a chest infection we called out the duty doctor for a home visit – bed-bound and hardly able to speak for coughing, Michael croaked 'How are you?' 'I rather think I should be asking you that question', she replied.

As I left the hospital later that evening, I would come across this young doctor crying and obviously quite traumatised on our account, being comforted by a senior colleague. It can't be easy to lose a patient, especially if you are new at the job. Why are patients who come into A&E with potentially very serious conditions not seen by at least one senior doctor with good diagnostic experience? These young doctors were charming and cheerful as they filled in all the requisite boxes on the forms, but how could they be expected to know that the man in front of them might be about to die? Someone with more years on the job might have been quicker on the uptake.

The second doctor decided to send Michael for a chest X-ray and a CT scan, though it took three more hours for the appropriate technicians to arrive at the hospital. During this time a friend came to take Ruairi away; he arrived at an awkward moment and flung open the curtain when I was trying to help Michael pee, which led to a spillage. There really is no dignity in hospital. In the confusion, Ruairi was scooped up and did not really say goodbye to his dad – yet another regret of mine, as he would only see him again as an inert figure strapped up to tubes and machines. But it is really no use to think this way; it isn't the final moments that count, but the lifetime of love that preceded them. And you don't say goodbye to someone every time as though it might be the last, although we do have a family rule, passed down from Michael's father, that you should never part in anger just in case.

From this moment on, things started to take a severely downward turn. I am composed of a strange mixture of optimism and pessimism (inherited from the personality extremes of my father and mother), so although I constantly anticipate and fear disaster there is a part of me that assumes things will turn out all right, no matter how bad they seem. It is still broadly my philosophy of life – that everything is for the best – but I've learned that sometimes things do have to get really terrible before they get to be OK. That afternoon things just kept getting worse and worse . . . and worse.

I had to help the nurse wheel the trolley through to the X-ray room. Where were all the porters? I had already assisted her in changing Michael's soaked sheets and, although it makes one feel better to be doing something, I wondered how our hospitals would function without relatives, and what it would be like if you were there alone. When my mother was taken into A&E a couple of years ago I waited with her the nine hours it took for a bed to become available so that they could admit her. In the next cubicle a very old lady of a hundred and something lay dying alone. She had been brought in by staff from the nursing home where she lived and lay on the trolley weakly calling out 'Nurse, nurse . . .' in a frightened voice. Of course nobody came, so finally I went to her bedside and held her hand for a while, telling her everything was going to be all right. Is this really how we should die?

Michael and I were left alone in the X-ray waiting-room and it was at this moment that the tension between us finally broke. Michael suddenly began to howl in fear; I howled too and we clung to each other, weeping. Two smartly-dressed African ladies in the waiting-room stared at us in obvious astonishment, which turned our tears to laughter. Michael reached over and patted me on the chest with his fist repeatedly and urgently: 'That's where I am – love, love, love! Remember . . . love!'

From the X-ray room we proceeded to the CT scan, though I had to wait outside. The results were shocking: he had a very large bleed on the right frontal lobe of his brain and we were told he would be transferred as soon as possible to the National Hospital for Neurology and Neurosurgery in Queen's Square, where they would operate. Later I was to learn that all this had been far from straightforward and the National had not wanted to accept him; an intensive-care nurse, a friend of ours, who was working at the first hospital that night, told me that she was expecting to admit him there. Bizarrely, the A&E registrar decided to pack him into an ambulance, unconscious at this stage, and send him off to the National anyway. The National could well have turned him away, except that by sheer luck there was a bed free and an operating team ready to go – all at 11 p.m. on a Sunday evening.

As I said, it's never just one thing that goes wrong: the mistakes and incompetencies pile up like a motorway crash. There are those you actually witness and those you only find out about later, like the fact that all Michael's notes were sent off in the ambulance with him and no copy kept, which of course made investigating what had happened much harder. (The National Hospital also managed to mislay his notes after he died there, which makes me wonder how commonly this must occur; it has certainly also happened once to me.) The behind-the-scenes scrabbling between the two hospitals over who would treat him only came to light a year later when I went through a complaints procedure.

Back in the waiting-room, it was when we got the results of the scan that Michael reminded me: 'This is how my mother died.' The story I knew was that Michael's mother had died at the age of forty-nine following a fall in which she banged her head; she had gone to bed as normal that night and then not woken up. She had had a lifetime of ill health, starting with rheumatic fever at the age of seventeen, which left her with a damaged heart. At the time of her death she had recently been given one of the earliest mitral-valve replacements; the loud clicking of this object in her chest scared her so much that she tried to blot it out with a dangerous cocktail of tranquillisers and alcohol.

For years Michael suspected his father of having played some part in his mother's death. Theirs was an explosive marriage, probably exacerbated by the fact that they were unable to have sex for most of it in case she became pregnant again. She had suffered congestive heart failure after both Michael's and his elder sister's births and been told by doctors that her heart would not stand another pregnancy. But for her, as a strict Catholic, birth control was out of the question. It seems rather as if anger took the place of sex as a release of tension between them; as a child Michael remembered cowering under the kitchen table, hearing his mother goad his father until he lashed out physically at her. Naturally he fell into a protective role towards his mother so that when she claimed that his dad had 'pushed her' he took this to mean that her fatal fall was somehow his father's doing. It took many years till his sister was able to convince him that his mother had been home alone when she fell.

But a brain haemorrhage – of course! Who knows now whether it might have been the bleeding that caused her to fall, rather than the other way around? Only later did I hear, from a cousin of Michael's, the whole story of the mother on life-support for six weeks while her grieving husband, children and sisters hoped and prayed around her bed; of the harrowing decision to switch off the machines and let her die. I wonder why I hadn't known this part before; I certainly knew about the nineteen-year-old Michael's dry-eyed fury at the funeral, of his descent into anorexia and psychosis the following year and the breakdown and suicide attempt while he was at graduate school in his early twenties. When I met him, aged twenty-nine, he was still on the slow climb back to stability – a fragile creature with scarred wrists, tormented by nightmares and sustained by music and poetry, and drinking. There were many things he could not, or would not, talk about until he learned to trust me.

Like many other things that happened during Michael's dying, this information seemed to come to me at a moment when it was most relevant. This was after all to be our story, though we didn't yet know it. We still thought, or at least I did, that he would be saved, cured, restored to a full and healthy life by medical intervention. We did manage, though, to have a brief conversation about death which I cherish, as I think it was really our goodbye – another of those moments of eternity when the truth shines through.

Michael had always feared death, even when I first knew him as a young man. I don't think a day passed when he didn't consider his own mortality, the possibility of non-existence. Losing his mother so young and then his father a few months after we met obviously compounded this fear, but I also wonder if he somehow knew inside that he would not make old bones, without knowing how or when he would die. That summer he had wondered aloud whether he had even ten years left: *'Timor mortis conturbat me,'* he said.

In my life, acquaintance with mortality has tended to come in waves. Turning forty I was confronted with a spate of sudden deaths: it began with a favourite aunt dying of cancer. Then there followed a friend's four-year-old daughter, of leukemia; the suicide of an assistant in Ruairi's kindergarten; a singing pupil of mine who died from a diabetic coma. They came thick and fast, about one a month over the year, culminating with the unexpected death of my father and another of my mother's sisters. I remembered that when I was a teenager my mother had to go to nine family funerals in a single year, perhaps when she was around the same age as I was now. When you enter your forties you are entering an 'age of grief', when things you have only read about or heard about start happening to those closest to you.

Recently, in the year before Michael's death, I had known or been connected to nine people who died of cancer in their forties or early fifties, including rather bizarrely the ex-husbands of two of my cousins. This time I had a strong feeling that I was being prepared for something: perhaps that particular disease, perhaps in myself or someone very close to me. Instead there was this.

I'm not suggesting that we can really know our future, although I have a firm conviction that I will die at the age of eighty-seven sitting quietly in my garden. But perhaps the body has its own wisdom and therefore maybe a foreknowledge of the longevity of the organism. Or perhaps constantly worrying, obsessing even, over your own demise contributes to ill health. Michael, like many young men, was slightly surprised to survive the age of thirty-three; it's a sort of Christ complex. In fact he did his best not to survive, slashing his wrists in a girlfriend's flat because he wanted to break up with her but didn't know how. Of course in romantic lore it behoves a poet to die tragically young, though there are many examples of elder-statesmen poets. Still, it is hard to imagine Michael, perennially child-like in many ways, a '*puer aeternus*', as a grizzled old man.

Now he started to speak quickly and urgently, issuing last instructions just in case. He told me that the poems he wanted published were in a computer file called 'Safest'; this was to become the title of the thin posthumous volume which we would publish the following year. 'Tell my friends to look after Ruairi, and keep up the fight.' What he dubbed the 'Poetry Wars', between the avant-garde academic faction and the more traditional (and popular) poets, had been Michael's obsession for several years. This is not the place to go into all the arguments, but he felt that everything he loved and fought for in his work – clarity, form, music, meaning – was being ridiculed and derided by the attacks of certain avant-garde writers, whom he dubbed 'the ampersands'. He feared for the posterity of his work, which he saw as being controlled by a small sector of the academic world.

'You'll be all right? I mean – there's enough money . . .?' I told him yes we'd be fine, although I really had no idea if this were true. You don't build up large reserves on a poet's salary and I currently had no income at all, having just finished my training course as an Alexander Technique teacher but having not yet begun looking for clients. Michael was functionally innumerate – the sort of person who when offered 'two for the price of one' would buy three – so I was always the one in charge of our finances. It was rather like the old-fashioned system whereby a man handed over his pay packet on a Friday night and his wife gave him pocket money for the weekend; everything operated out of my bank account and I simply asked him to transfer money when necessary. I also handled the financial side of his career; otherwise he would hardly ever have got paid, as sending out invoices seemed somehow beyond him.

I had always worked, even when Ruairi was a baby, except for the past year when I was in my final year of teacher-training; I realised I was finding it impossible to be an effective student, mother and teacher all at the same time. But I had never earned very much whereas, although Michael had only a low income from readings and teaching and – despite their success – nothing worth speaking of in royalty payments for his books, he did occasionally win substantial prizes and grants. So he was a sort of meal ticket with the occasional banquet thrown in. I wasn't sure how we would manage without him, but I wasn't going to start troubling him with financial worries at this point. It has been my experience that life provides what you need in unexpected ways, which would be borne out subsequently.

I realised we were talking about death, without actually talking about it. I looked him in the eye: 'Do you think this is it? I mean, deep down inside yourself?' 'I don't know,' he answered. The big 'it', the one we had both been waiting for. Because beneath the shock, the unreality, the uncertainty, I seemed to recognise what was happening. It was what I had subconsciously been preparing for all along, just as all of your life there is a subtle preparation for losing your parents.

In some deep part of me I knew for certain that Michael would die before me and that it would most likely be in this manner: the emergency ambulance; the hospital; a sudden and brutal snatching away. Not that either of us was expecting it quite yet – he was only fifty, for God's sake. Maybe this was just one more false alarm ...

Back in the wretched cubicle Michael's condition began to deteriorate suddenly and alarmingly. I have never got to the bottom of this, owing to the lost notes fiasco and to the fact that a post-mortem was not performed; apparently it's almost impossible to tell the course of events after a brain haemorrhage has occured. Was the initial bleed still continuing, gradually worsening the intra-cranial pressure, or did he have a re-bleed at some point? His face began to droop on the left side and his speech to slur as he repeatedly told me how much he loved me and Ruairi. He complained of nausea and an unbearable headache; the nurse, who was the only person we could get hold of, gave him painkillers and an anti-emetic, which seemed rather like sticking a Band-Aid on a severed limb. I can't complain about the nurse, though, as throughout the day she had clearly been keeping a weather eye on Michael and was probably the only person with enough experience to realise the severity of his situation.

Gradually he began to lose consciousness, his eyes drooping and fluttering and panic setting in: 'Doctor!' he pleaded in a desperate voice and I stroked his head and found myself saying, rather strangely, 'Mummy's here.' He then seemed to pass out and I called his name sharply, asking him to give me a sign that he could still hear me. He made a scrabbling motion with his hands, plucking at the bedclothes; my father had done this during his last night of life, and apparently my grandfather also. I wonder if it is a common occurrence, a last clinging on to life. Then he was gone, and I think effectively brain-dead from this moment on, though it would be several days before his body followed suit.

Suddenly the hospital was all action: the resuscitation team rushed in, the trolley with Michael on it was whisked out of my sight and I was ushered into the 'relatives' room', a modern strip-lit cube with a fish tank and a couple of blue sofas, tucked well away from the main action. The door was shut on me, and for more than an hour nobody came near. I kept expecting someone to walk in and say: 'I'm sorry . . .' Eventually I found the buzzing silence intolerable and went back into the A&E to find somebody to tell me what was happening. There were no staff in sight, as usual, so I marched into the resuscitation unit where I found Michael stretched out naked on a gurney like an experimental animal, with tubes inserted into every orifice. The young medics were joking about the hectic nature of the evening's case-load; they saw me and pulled the curtain across, telling me firmly to go away.

The registrar appeared and admonished me: 'Your husband is very seriously ill – he may die!' As if all this were somehow my fault. 'We're trying to stabilise him for the transfer. Please go and wait in the relatives' room, and I will let you know when we're ready to leave.' I took one peek back into the empty cube with its illuminated fish tank, and instead took myself outside to make more phone calls, huddled in the dim light from the doorway of the ambulance bay. How I needed my friends now. One, a trained nurse, is something of a health help-line service for us all; nobody was telling me anything and I valued her calm and knowledgeable input. I completely forgot that it was her birthday.

Eventually Michael was loaded into the ambulance and I was told there would not be room for me with all the people and equipment trying to keep him alive. I didn't feel capable of driving and the idea of taking a taxi alone through the dark was awful. Luckily a close friend came up trumps: she had just driven back from Bristol and must have been exhausted, but she agreed immediately to come and get me and take me down to the National Hospital. Ruairi would spend the night at his friend's house and be taken into school the next day.

All this took a long time – it was several hours before they got Michael into the ambulance, and of course there was the wrangling about whether the National would take him, which I didn't know about. The young doctor who had been moved by our plight gripped my arm, her eyes full of tears: 'Let us know what happens.' I had to move my car out of the hospital car park where it would probably get clamped, and on to the street. Then I stumbled down the hill to where I had agreed to meet my friend and on impulse ran into McDonald's for a burger and chips. I usually turn my nose up at this kind of food but that night it was a welcome sight. I hadn't eaten all day except for a couple of chocolate bars and too many cups of tea, and I was shaking with hunger, fatigue and terror.

CHAPTER 2

It was gone eleven when we arrived at the National Hospital for Neurology and Neurosurgery in Queen's Square to find the reception in semi-darkness and nobody around. I was so very glad to be arriving with someone, rather than alone. The night porter took a long time to find out where Michael was – again I had the constant dread that I might be about to hear bad news – but finally we were sent up to the fifth floor and shown into another relatives' room: a big L-shaped space with, at least, facilities for making tea and coffee. (This hospital also had its little strip-lit cube – no fish tank this time – which I would visit several times over the week. I came to call it the Bad News Room.)

A nurse came in to tell us that Michael was being taken straight into surgery, which would probably last a couple of hours. At this point she was relatively upbeat, although she did explain that they had not been expecting him. Not long afterwards, though, she returned to say that she had had a look at the scans and she thought we should prepare for the worst; the haemorrhage had been very severe. My friend and I didn't take to her at all – we thought her gloomy and pessimistic, as indeed she was, but not without reason as it turned out.

When you are in the middle of this kind of crisis you think that all you want is the truth, but what you really want is hope. I had been part of this drama already since the morning; my friend was a more recent arrival. But neither of us was ready to hear that Michael might not survive. This hospital, however, was prepared for our ambivalence, and consummately skilled in dealing with it. Over the coming days they would gently steer me towards acceptance of the truth, acceptance of death, combined with an even more gentle acknowledgement that we all need to keep faith in miracles. Michael's pupils were not reactive, a sign of brain death, even before the surgery, and the operation almost didn't go ahead. I think the surgeons knew that they probably couldn't save him but they operated because they could; because he was father of a young child; because it was a last chance.

A young member of the surgical team came to explain the procedure: they would slice open the top of the skull and try to drain the blood. He warned us that operating on the brain was in itself a traumatising intervention. The recovery process would be very slow and there might well be permanent damage. I didn't really hear all the bad stuff about brain damage; I grabbed at the word 'recovery' and clung to it. Michael, for all his hypochondria, was as strong as an ox, with what my son calls 'Irish muscles', built for navvying. He had been apparently at death's door on previous occasions and survived; surely this was just one more close call? I was allowed into the corridor as they brought him through on a trolley, to give him a quick kiss and squeeze his hand.

Both my friend and I were beside ourselves with tension and exhaustion. We roamed giddily around the waiting-room making and then discarding cups of tea, then huddled together under a blanket on the plastic couch. The lights in the room were dimmed but there was illumination from the street lights through the large uncurtained windows. I can't remember what we talked about but I think we laughed with slight hysteria a few times.

At about 2 a.m. the surgeon came to tell us that he had done what he could and that the next two days would be crucial, during which Michael would be kept under sedation to allow the swelling in his brain to subside. The surgeon seemed to us to be satisfied with the operation and optimistic about recovery, although this may have been what we wanted to hear; or perhaps he was just buzzing with adrenalin from the surgery. There was nothing to do but go home and wait. My friend took me back to collect my car at the first hospital and then followed me home, coming in with me to make sure I was all right.

Thus began one of the strangest, and longest, weeks of my life. I slept late the next day and rang the hospital immediately I woke to hear that there had been no change, significantly no response in the pupils. But Michael was still sleeping it off, I told myself, and he was always a very deep sleeper. At this point I must have rung one of his close friends because the news ran round the poetry network like wildfire. Messages of support came in: prayers were being said for him, from Catholic masses to Buddhist chants. Everyone said he would survive; he was strong; he would fight. I wasn't so sure: I knew he was stoic about pain but could you call him a fighter? We had a joke between us that if our plane crashed in the Andes, as in the story *Alive!*, he would most likely lie down in the snow and give up whereas I would be hunting around for people to eat, probably including him.

I called the hospital several times during the day but things were still the same. My best friend took the day off work and came over to keep me company and in the afternoon we picked up Ruairi from school and took him in to the hospital to see his daddy. Michael had a bandage cap covering his head, and a tube draining saliva from his mouth, which made him look slightly grotesque. He was hooked up to numerous machines with beeps and flashing lights, which interested Ruairi more than the inert unresponsive figure on the bed, who looked like he was sleeping except that you couldn't wake him up. In the event we stayed less than an hour; it was clearly too strange and traumatic for Ruairi and he got bored and restless. I also didn't feel there was much I could do by mounting a bedside vigil. My friend brought us home and cooked dinner, accompanied by strong gin-and-tonics and chocolate.

The next morning a carpenter arrived to build shelves in my newly-decorated teaching room. I had almost forgotten he was coming but there seemed no point in cancelling at this stage; good workmen are hard to get hold of in London. I later found out that his wife was a bereavement counsellor, which seemed weirdly appropriate. Leaving him in the house to get on with equipping my uncertain future, I went down to the National and sat by Michael's bed all day. On my way from the Tube to Queen's Square I passed a discount book shop where I bought a picture book of Frida Kahlo's paintings, wondering if it was somehow immoral to be shopping when your husband was unconscious in hospital. Kahlo's paintings have become linked in my mind to that time, particularly the one of her four-poster bed floating in the sky; her sleeping form draped in a bright yellow blanket, and on top of the canopy a skeleton.

My sister had wanted to come up straight away on Sunday, but I told her to hold off until I really needed her. Eight years earlier she had been due to be my birthing companion, but Ruairi arrived so precipitately that, although she was on her way, she just missed his arrival. In the event, this was probably for the best, as Michael had been my only companion for most of the labour, rather than taking a back seat. Now I knew she would be there to support me through my husband's last days and beyond. But first I needed some time alone to adjust to what was happening, so I asked her to plan on coming the next day, promising I would summon her urgently if things changed for the worse.

In the way that time has of slowing down when you are *in extremis*, those four days of vigil by Michael's bedside in the National seemed to last for months. But now I think of them as a kind of gift: time for me to catch up; say goodbye; let go. If he had died Sunday night in the A&E, after such an appalling day, things would have felt very different.

What happened during that long Tuesday was essentially a shift of perspective. To begin with I assumed that I was waiting for some change to occur, a sign of healing or Michael returning to consciousness. I had my first meeting (in the Bad News Room) with a wonderful consultant with whom I would speak several times over the following days; he had a marvellous gift of really listening to what you said, hearing what it was you wanted to know, and giving carefully considered, thoughtful replies. My experience is that many doctors, particularly busy hospital ones, simply tell you what they think you need to hear or what they have decided, speaking in the royal 'we'. This consultant told me they still had Michael under sedation and would gradually reduce it over the next twenty-four hours, then we would see what happened.

I have thought a lot about why my experience at this hospital was so different from the first A&E. Was it because as a specialist hospital they were under less pressure; had better resources; attracted the most qualified and experienced staff? But a hospital can be medically efficient without necessarily being a humane environment. There was something in the ethos of the National that treated everyone – the patients, the relatives, and I hope also the staff – as profoundly human. I never saw the nurses perform any procedure on Michael without asking his permission and apologising for the discomfort, even though he was deeply unconscious and apparently unaware of everything. I wonder if it is because they are dealing with the brain, which is so much the locus of personality: the spirit rather than the machine. As the consultant said, we know almost all there is to know about the functioning (and malfunctioning) of the heart and other organs, but of the brain's workings we still understand only a tiny fraction. It's the medical challenge of the future.

That day as I sat beside Michael's bed trying but failing to read the novel I had started on holiday the week before, looking at my Frida Kahlo paintings, I came to understand several things. I realised how easily one could get attached to that familiar body on the ventilator, to all intents and purposes alive and breathing but peacefully asleep and cared for by professionals, rather than awake and needing your attention. Your life would quickly become a ritual of visits to the silent form in the hospital bed and of course there would always be the hope of it coming round. The doctor had told me that after a few weeks on the machines the autonomic brain function does appear to improve slightly, maybe leading to involuntary movements which give the (false) impression that the person is regaining consciousness. The hospital do their best to gently move you on from such an attachment, not I think for any reasons of finance or convenience for them but because they believe it is not fair to either the patient or the family to create false hope.

These are the strange dilemmas of modern medical tech-nology: we are able to keep a person alive beyond their own capabilities so that decisions have to be made which either prolong or terminate their existence. Sometimes, as happened to a friend's father, the breathing support is withdrawn but the person lives on, brain-dead, and it becomes a question of withholding nourishment or even water to bring about their end. I was glad that Michael and I had married the year before as it meant I was in a position to make decisions on his behalf, such as not to resuscitate him if his heart failed. Without this permission they would have been obliged to try everything to keep him alive.

Some people would say we play God with our machines and our life-or-death decisions, but it comes down to this: we may have the technology but I don't believe the outcomes are in our control. Just as when I was trying to get pregnant, I had to resort to *in vitro* fertilisation; well, you can bring the egg and sperm together so they rub noses in a test-tube but nothing can force them to unite and grow into a baby. That is still the big mystery.

Besides, although I talked away to Michael throughout the day – explaining what had happened in case he was in some dark, confused place inside that bandaged head; telling him my love for him and apologising for not taking him seriously at first and being so angry – although I spoke to his face, to his ears, I gradually began to feel that he – 'he' – was not there. I remembered visiting my dad's body an hour or so after he had died. I was very scared as, at forty, I'd never seen a dead person before, but a wise nurse told me that if it's someone you loved, it isn't at all frightening. And at first he seemed just like my daddy asleep, although more calm than in life, when there would be the snuffling and fidgeting and his disconcertingly noisy breathing. But it was as though while I sat there an emptiness came over the room and I realised that this body was just the vessel that had contained my father, which he had now deserted. Michael, being brought up a Catholic, had seen many dead people laid out for visiting at the wake and he always said: 'They're not in there.'

Michael's body was still alive, his chest rising and falling with the ventilator, but other than that there were no signs of life: no sounds; no response when I squeezed his hand or stroked his head. The continuation of his body was measured in beeps and rising and falling banks of coloured lights. I didn't feel he had gone away completely, but simply that he was no longer inside that body that I was talking to. I persisted, though, because I'd read that hearing is the last sense to go, though I do wonder how on earth they know.

When I was at school a girl in my class was knocked down by a car and lay brain-damaged in a coma for months. We took turns to visit and talk to her about school and our lives, or about music, which was her passion. It was extremely odd, talking to an unresponsive body, but the doctors thought that she might still be able to hear and that our talking might help to bring her round, which was what eventually happened. And in the film *The Diving Bell and the Butterfly*, based on a true story, the protagonist suffers from 'locked-in syndrome' after a stroke: his mind still functions perfectly but he cannot move a muscle except for the ability to blink one eyelid. He laboriously dictates a book about his experiences to an assistant by blinking to signal which letter of the alphabet he wishes to use next.

But Michael didn't seem to be locked in but rather let out. During this week a number of people who hadn't heard that he was ill had vivid dreams about him and one told me much later of a kind of waking fantasy where he appeared at her door in a dishevelled state, saying: 'I'm OK but you've got to help Maddy – she's in terrible trouble.' (At this time she had no idea that he was in hospital, but she would later be instrumental in my getting a charitable grant from a fund for supporting writers' families.) It makes a strange kind of sense to me that a man who loved and was loved by so many people might spend his last days on earth trying to connect with as many as possible.

There are many different traditions regarding the length of time a soul stays attached to the body: Buddhism, for example, says it is three days. That is why in many religious practices the body is kept at home while friends and relatives sit with it; although there are also many religions, particularly those originating in hot countries, in which the body is dealt with as quickly as possible. For a while I was troubled by this: if someone had died but was kept alive on machines, where was their soul? But I'm pretty sure I know what Michael's was up to: out networking through the ether.

As I left the hospital that evening I got into the lift and burst into tears. Two women asked me what was wrong and when I told them my husband was dying they took me down to the café in the basement and bought me a cake and cup of tea – again all I'd had to eat all day. It's almost impossible to think of eating when you are digesting such an enormous event in your life. Despite the best efforts of friends to feed me, I lost over a stone in the following month.

I arrived home to more messages of support and positive thinking and realised that during that day I had moved into a different space. I wasn't yet convinced Michael would die – after all, there are sometimes miraculous recoveries – but what was clear to me now was that it was no longer in my, or anyone else's, hands. We could wish and hope and urge all we wanted; we could perform sophisticated medical procedures; but ultimately what would be, would be.

More than that, we needed to let him go, to set him free. A sixty-year-old grandmother from Essex had been brought into the hospital after Michael, also with a brain haemorrhage, and what looked like her entire clan, including grandchildren, had turned out to sit by her bed in rotation, pretty much commandeering the relatives' room. Even after her life-support machines were switched off she remained alive but she was still unconscious when we left the hospital. I don't know the eventual outcome but I had the feeling that there was no way this family was going to let her go gently. Sometimes I wondered was it love, drama, or simply a family 'three-line whip' that brought them all there? And did I give up too easily? Should I have held on longer, praying for a miracle?

That night I hardly slept. After a fitful hour or so in bed I got up and made phone calls to friends in America, taking advantage of the time difference. Around 5 a.m. I went back to bed and dreamed that Michael and I were in Spain or somewhere warm. It was a balmy evening and we were on an old stone terrace with some kind of classical portico; he looked young and well in a bright orange T-shirt, and he took me in his arms, saying that he was all right and everything would be fine. I became aware of a figure lying in a bed off to the side and said to Michael: 'But what about that fellow over there?' to which he replied:

'Oh, it's time for him to go now.' It was at this moment that the phone rang. The nurse – the same one who had been on duty the night we came in – told me that Michael's heart rhythm was very unstable and I should come in immediately. She said she thought he was waiting for me. (I later learned that she had lost a boyfriend to brain cancer when they were both very young.)

Although it was very early in the morning I quickly rang a couple of people: a wise older female friend, facilitator of the reading group I attended, who had been giving me moral and spiritual support through this week, and the friend who had come with me to the hospital on Sunday night and who volunteered to come and drive us down there again and then take Ruairi to spend the day with her daughter, who was his best friend. I also rang my sister, telling her that she should come quickly.

I knew what I had to do next, which was tell Ruairi that his dad was probably going to die. Up to this point I had simply said that he was very ill and the doctors were trying to help him get better. This must rank as about the worst thing I have ever had to do in my life: you want nothing more than to protect and keep your children safe and then you must be the agent of their pain and sorrow; must wake them from sleep to tell them unbearably awful news. The moment the words were out of my mouth I wanted to call them back, pretend it was just a cruel joke. Ruairi sobbed: 'Not my daddy!' He was trembling, his teeth chattering, from being dragged awake so early and from the shock. He said: 'I've been afraid that something like this would happen ever since his heart went wrong', and it shook me to realise what a heavy load of anxiety this eight-year-old boy had been carrying around. But Michael's own anxiety had been a palpable energy in our household, and of course Ruairi had picked up on it.

He then said that he didn't want to go to the funeral or even to school, and I could see his desperation, his yearning for things to be normal, not to be marked out as the boy whose father has died. Or perhaps he was just feeling what I had felt in the A&E: a foreboding of how hard this journey was going to be and an unwillingness for it to start. As I helped him dress and lace up his shoes he said grimly: 'Life isn't going to be any fun any more – who will play "Cat and Rat" with me?' (a game Michael and he had devised together about a pair of animal detectives). 'And we didn't finish writing our book.' Michael and Ruairi were always at play on some project together: a story-book with drawings; an imaginary game with a complex cast of characters. Ruairi was right: I wouldn't be able to do all that with him, being one of those adults who doesn't really know how to play. It's commonly said that dads are better at playing with children while mothers usually feel they have something else they should be doing, but this went beyond the usual physical rough-and-tumble. Michael and Ruairi shared a very special inner world.

One of Ruairi's guinea-pigs had died a few months previously. I remember coming into the kitchen that morning and putting the kettle on, then suddenly having a strong feeling that something in the room wasn't quite right. It's fascinating how our nervous systems pick up information about what is going on even when our thoughts are elsewhere: a sort of 'hyper-sensory' perception. When I looked in the cage I found the little guinea-pig, Winnie, already stiff and cold. Part of the rationale for keeping pets is that it helps teach children about death. This had certainly been the case for me when my dog was run over outside my house; I was thirteen and grieved profoundly for months, far more than I would for my grandparents. Now Ruairi groaned: 'This is just like when Winnie died, only worse.' And it was.

While waiting for my friend to pick us up we wrote a little letter to the angels asking them to keep Michael safe and, Ruairi insisted on adding, bring him back to us. We burned it in the living-room fireplace as we do every year with our wishes for the

New Year. I have no specific religious belief but this isn't to say I have no sense of the numinous; using ideas of angels and heaven to support my child, and myself, at this time seemed perfectly right. These kinds of symbols would play a big part in our surviving the coming weeks and months. In a society which avoids even thinking of death, which almost regards it as a tragic mistake at whatever age, most of us no longer have the structures, either religious or social, to contain the extremes of feeling that the crossing of this threshold invokes. It falls to us as individuals to try and develop our own rituals of reassurance, our own rites of passage.

It is at once a freedom and a burden: cutting loose from time-worn rules for living in society means we have to make up our lives as we go along. I remember when Ruairi was a baby how I longed for someone to tell me what to do, be it four-hourly feeds and a nap at the bottom of the garden or whatever. Instead I had to make choices every step of the way, wondering always whether I was getting it right. On the other hand I am a rule-breaker, a determined non-joiner, so I daresay I would have balked at any regime imposed from outside. At least there were plenty of books of 'expert' advice on parenting, to be followed or disregarded. When it comes to death, though, once you have left behind orthodox religious approaches there is precious little in the way of support.

By the time we got to the hospital that morning Michael's heart rate had settled down a bit, although there were occasional nerve-racking gaps indicated by that long uninterrupted bleep of the monitor that always signifies death in TV programmes. The sedation he'd been under for two days was now being withdrawn, which may explain the sudden volatility of his condition. By now I was certain that it was only a question of time before he would die. I told Ruairi that he needed to say goodbye because he would probably not see daddy again and lifted him up to kiss the strange unshaven sleeping face with its mouth distorted by tubes. With his usual buoyancy Ruairi asked for a bag of Maltesers 'to cheer us up' and fed one to Michael as one would to a doll or a teddy, holding it briefly to his lips. Then my friend took him off to her house for breakfast and I settled in by the bedside.

My sister arrived and I realised straight away that, coming into the situation at this stage, it might take her a while to find her way to the point of acceptance that I had already reached. She practises a form of hands-on healing and immediately put her hand to Michael's forehead, saying she could feel a lot of 'commotion' in there. The rest of that morning felt rather strange and confusing, with my sister acting as if there was still hope he would recover and me already reconciled to losing him.

We were ushered out of the ward while the doctors made their rounds; this angered me at first until they explained that it was for the privacy of the other patients. Then we were shown into the Bad News Room to talk to the lovely – and strangely beautiful, with a long neck and piercing blue eyes – consultant I had met the day before. I told him of my dream and he said it was important because I would always remember it. He told us they would wait a further twenty-four hours after stopping the sedation to 'give him a chance to see what he could do alone'. Michael had apparently taken over a little of the breathing, which indicated that his brainstem was not completely destroyed; breathing and coughing are reflex functions. However there was no sign of higher-brain activity, since his pupils were still completely non-reactive (this was checked at regular intervals throughout the day).

I asked the nurse if I could lie on the bed and cuddle Michael. By now, after several days on intravenous fluids, his hands felt stiff and swollen so that you couldn't really hold them properly any more. The nurse and I carefully moved him over to one side of the bed and lowered it so that I could climb on, then she pulled a curtain around us. I'm not sure what I had hoped for from this experience but it was rather like lying next to – well, a corpse, or one of those dummies used for practising the kiss of life. I could feel his weight pressing against me, taking up all of the mattress as he had in bed at home. Being so close-up to this unresponsive figure was quite disturbing. Maybe he didn't like it either as it was only a minute or two before the monitors began emitting distress signals and I had to leap down and run to find the nurse, thinking I might have killed him.

My sister and I went for lunch in a nearby café with a friend of Michael's who was acting as my liaison with the outside world, or at least the poetry part of it. He had popped into the ward very briefly but said he didn't really want to spend time there; none of Michael's close friends seemed to want to join the bedside vigil, which I was thankful for. It was hard enough dealing with my own emotions at this point. I told him he should let people know that, although Michael was still alive, the outlook was bleak. Later in the day as we were heading home, we stopped off at Sainsbury's to buy something for supper. Being out in the world and trying to do normal things felt so strange, like being very ill and feverish, or wading through syrup. A young father in front of me took his little boy up into his arms and I had to abandon my basket and run from the shop in tears.

Standing on the escalator as it descended into the Under-ground, I had a vision of myself tumbling the whole way down to the bottom. It seemed preposterous to be getting on the tube while Michael lay dying. We had bought some expensive bubble bath – our version of Ruairi's Maltesers, perhaps – and my sister and I both had a bath to try and relax. That night I used my sleepless hours to research funerals on the internet, feeling somehow that I was being slightly treacherous, or jumping the gun. But I knew what was coming.

I woke, after little sleep, to what I knew would be Michael's last day. After a friend had picked up Ruairi to take him to school my sister and I loitered around at home drinking tea and talking, reluctant to start the day. I remember moving very slowly and carefully as though everything required extra thought and effort to accomplish; even our voices seemed quieter. I felt quite calm although with an ache of dread, almost as though I were facing my own execution. Eventually there was nothing to do but get dressed and get on the Underground to the hospital.

This should have been one of the worst days of my life and in retrospect it takes on that quality, so much so that I am almost afraid to write of it. But in some ways it was also one of the finest – a day that brought me closer than I have ever been to some kind of raw truth about life. As all outside concerns fell away – home, food, other people – what was happening right there in the hospital took on an intensely real aspect. The three days I had spent in there had already seemed an eternity, and my journey from hope and anxiety to acceptance and release had slowed time to a crawl. Was this what people sometimes experience when they are in extreme danger: a sense of calm, of knowing exactly what to do, of having all the time in the world? Perhaps it's one of the effects of adrenalin, that it protects you for a while by giving you a tremendous sense of strength and focused attention.

I was about to watch my beloved husband, my companion of twenty-one years, the person I had effectively grown up with for my whole adult life, be allowed to die. How could it be OK? And yet, in a strange way, that's how it felt, as though we had come to some sort of inevitable resolution. When a student of mine was dying of lymphoma, he described his transfer to hospital during the final crisis as 'the relief of limited choices'. It was out of my, or anyone else's, hands – this was the end of a cycle. Even in that high-tech environment with all the machines and monitors, it had about it the physical inexorability of birth: the earthiness of blood, sweat, breath, flesh.

Perhaps if you work at meditation for a lifetime, or are born with a luckily phlegmatic constitution, you experience more moments like this of being in the eternal present, of everything being just as it should be. For me, and I think for many others, the experience comes in unexpected flashes, triggered by the extremes in life and more usually the extremes of crisis rather than of joy. It is an awakening to life in its fullness, a sense of being more completely alive than you have ever felt, which you might call 'awe'. I would mourn this absolute clarity once life returned to its more usual sense of a chaotic muddle.

At our last interview in the Bad News Room that day the possibility of organ donation was raised. They were not interested in his heart and lungs because he was already brain-dead, but they might be able to use his liver and kidneys, and also his corneas. I agreed to meet with the donor coordinator later that morning. I had always considered organ donation to be a Good Thing; a close friend of mine works with liver transplant patients and Michael's own sister is a kidney dialysis nurse. So I was taken aback by my own ambivalence about allowing Michael to be cut up and bits of him taken away, even if they might give life to another. Also, I wondered whether his organs would be in a usable state, given the various abuses he had subjected them to; I had an irrational fear that they might take one look and turn up their noses. And as for the corneas, well, Michael was a very beautiful man, with eyes of a startling rich grey-blue colour. Somehow I couldn't bear the thought of giving them away.

I struggled with this head–heart dilemma all morning. No help from the man himself – the only donor card he carried read 'I want to help necrophiliacs find pleasure after my death.' I learned from the coordinator, who did not spare me any grim details, that a member of the transplant team would need to be present at his death and that we would have only a couple of minutes with the body before they would take him away and operate to remove the organs; there was no time to lose. Michael had just had his gall-bladder out in May that year and now here he was hooked up again to all manner of instruments and tubes.

I realised that I wanted – needed – him to be left alone and to die in peace and whole.

There was a very special nursing sister on the ward that day, a woman of great experience and commitment who elected to stay with us until the end, even though her shift had ended hours before. She suggested that we might like to have some mementos – handprints, a lock of hair. We messed around for a while, inking up Michael's swollen hands and trying to get a good impression on the paper, eventually coming up with something satisfactory. It hangs on the wall by Ruairi's bed reminding me of the cave-art handprints that survive from prehistoric times; you can put your own hand up against it and feel you are making contact with something eternal. It also recalls the hand- and footprints we made of Ruairi as a little baby – impossibly tiny, a record of a fleeting stage of his, and our, life.

The lock of hair, filthy and stiff by now, we cut and put in a small plastic bag: again an echo of the golden curl of Ruairi's baby hair that I keep in my memory box along with the clip from the umbilical cord and his first lost tooth. Now I wonder why we don't take photographs of the dead, or even make a death mask? I'm sure this sounds gruesome and is probably not the way one would like to be remembered, although it used to be common. My favourite uncle, who died of cancer, did not want us to visit him in his final weeks, out of a sense of shame about what he was, quite literally, reduced to. So I didn't take pictures or even draw any, which is another way I have of committing things to memory, but the image of Michael's comatose face, his mouth pulled rather grotesquely down on one side by the tubes, is burned on my retina as clearly as any photograph. Recently at the dentist's with Ruairi I had to turn away as I watched him fitted with a similar drain-tube; I thought for a moment I might faint, so strongly does the past leap out to ambush you.

We left the hospital to have lunch and meet up with a close friend of Michael's who lived nearby. Her sister's husband had died a year previously, leaving her with two small children; I regarded her as one of my guides to the path I was embarking on. These little forays out of the hospital were exceedingly strange and disorientating, like waking briefly from a dream to real life. On the way back we visited the hospital chapel; I suppose most hospitals have them, but this was a particularly beautiful one, with a constant supply of little candles which you could light. I had sat there more than once already; on one occasion someone was practising a Beethoven piano sonata on the old piano, but most often I was the only one in there and it provided a little sanctuary of calm in which to think and, I suppose, pray, if that is what it was.

I don't really remember the rest of that afternoon except to say that preparations continued: the transfer to the side ward, where we washed and dressed Michael in readiness for his final journey. There were no more conferences in the Bad News Room now we all knew what was coming, but I did not feel either rushed or at all frightened. I think it was at this point I had a long talk to Michael, telling him what was going to happen: that we were going to take him off the ventilator and that he had a choice to take over the breathing and fight for life (which I'm not sure he did), but that if he did it would be a very long and difficult recovery, probably never complete. I had been shown the scans of his brain and the blood clot covered almost entirely one half of it, radiating out from the area that is thought to be responsible for creativity, almost as though his 'poetry brain' had burst. Not only was this area substantially destroyed, but the rest of the brain had been badly crushed by the pressure of the blood pooling inside the skull. The damage was huge and irreversible.

We had a final cup of tea in the basement cafeteria and then came up to the ward to finish things.

'Our Life Stories' . . .

I met Michael on a street corner in Chicago when I was twenty-five. He was four years older and was still officially in graduate school there, although by then he had more or less deserted his PhD in favour of playing music. I'd come to Chicago in pursuit of another man, a neuroscientist whom I met on a back-packing trip around America; I had moved in with him but the relationship was doomed – we were simply too different. It was the first time I had ever allowed myself to fall in love and when it ended I was in pieces, but a door had been opened in my heart; I see now that the result of that first love affair was to put me in position, both geographically and emotionally, to meet Michael.

The day we met, he was playing the tin whistle in his Irish band 'Samradh Music' at a street fair, and I was working – one of several cash-in-hand jobs I had picked up – distributing leaflets for a local shop. I positioned myself at the edge of the audience and took advantage of the crowd to give out my leaflets; I liked Irish music and had gone out with a traditional flute player when I lived in France. Michael had thick curly hair, incredibly long eyelashes and an expression of rapturous absorption in the music, and my first impression was that he looked like trouble: my kind of trouble, though, with his slightly ethereal beauty and air of romance. I didn't yet know that he wrote poetry, but at the age of sixteen I had told my mother I would marry a poet and live in a garret; I knew my own romantic nature.

I hung around after the performance and introduced myself to the band members. I had just cut my own hair rather badly, and Michael said later that I reminded him of a lost baby bird. He recognised my name and asked if I was on their mailing list – it turned out that we had both read articles the other had written for the university arts journal (mine was a review of a book called On the Problem of Men, his a piece about a trip to Belfast) and that we lived just round the corner from each other. But it took some *pursuit on my part to bring us together; I tracked him down at another gig the following weekend, but he had to dash off to work afterwards. He worked most nights as a doorman in a North Side apartment building, coming home on public transport at a dangerous hour of the morning – he liked the peacefulness of the job, but not the necessary subservience. I made discreet enquiries of his housemates and turned up at his house for dinner on his evening off, when it was his turn to cook. Later he walked me home. He was always so warm and friendly in his dealings with everyone that it was hard to know whether his feelings went beyond geniality; one friend warned me that he was friends with a lot of women, but she didn't know whether he had girlfriends.*

But then he asked to come in; we kissed in the glow of a blue light-bulb in my living-room and thus began our history together. His heart had also been badly broken in a recent relationship so we trod carefully at first, but fell very quickly into a kind of desperate love. We knew we would only have the summer together, as my American visa was expiring and I had plans to meet up with a friend in Delhi and travel round India: the sort of 'meet on a certain day at a certain time' plans that pre-dated mobile phones and email. By the time I left Chicago, I was convinced we should be together, though I couldn't quite foresee how or where.

My trip to India was haunted by almost constant dreams of America and Michael, from which I would awaken to morning in an Indian hotel with a sense of shock and displacement. Within three months I fell ill with hepatitis, a disease that I'd noticed often beset travellers when they were in some confusion or doubt about their journey, and I decided to abandon the trip and return home as soon as I was well enough to travel. In the meantime I got a poste-restante letter from Michael, delayed by several weeks, saying that his father, whom I had met briefly in New York, had died suddenly of a heart attack in his sixties. Michael was sinking into grief and depression; I knew I had to get back to America and be with him.

As soon as I could, I returned to England and then Chicago and moved into Michael's basement room in a funky old communal house that had apparently once been lived in by members of the Weather Underground. We had very different domestic standards, and learning to live together, even in a shared house, was not easy; he was very put out when I took it upon myself to alphabetise his poetry bookshelf, even though I found a missing hundred dollars in the process. He had already published a few poems in magazines and during this time began to work on putting together his first collection of poems, which had been commissioned by a former girlfriend who worked in publishing. He would sit working into the night while I slept in an alcove, on the brand new sheets he had bought in my honour. Meanwhile, I worked at various babysitting and cleaning jobs, and spent weekends trailing around with Michael to Irish music gigs, sitting around with the other band members' partners while the band rehearsed and sound-checked.

Determined to exhibit my own musical credentials, I started learning the tin whistle; I found it difficult at first to remember the tunes, as I was used to reading music, and Irish music is largely played by ear. I also briefly took up playing a piano accordion which I had bought at a local flea market – I never really got the hang of the bellows and it occasionally wheezed horribly. I had always been keen on writing, so I joined a women's poetry group and continued to contribute articles to the student arts journal. Michael was at that time poetry editor of the prestigious Chicago Review, but of course I never dared submit anything there; on the one occasion I shyly showed him a love poem I had written for him, he proceeded to critique it.

After six months my visa expired once more and I decided to leave Chicago and pursue a Women's Studies MA in England, the prospectus for which I had come across in the offices of the feminist student group I was involved with. By now I had a close network of women friends in Chicago whom I had met through this group, but I felt stubbornly that I did not want to simply attach my life

39

to Michael's and that it was time to make my own career choices. Besides, for me to be able to stay and work in the States we would have to get married, an institution which Michael opposed even more vehemently than I did, and which anyway would have seemed a rather premature step.

So once again I left and returned to London, where I found a room in a shared flat, got a part-time job and started my MA course. In my mind we were still a couple, although for a year and a half we conducted our relationship from separate continents by means of long and frustrating phone calls – I remember the annoying way your own voice would echo back at you, obscuring the other person's response, and the sound of costly 'call units' ticking over during uncomfortable silences – and a couple of short and thrilling transatlantic visits. It certainly kept the romantic tension alive, but was overall a miserable and lonely experience, fraught with uncertainty. I really wanted Michael to come to London and live with me, but I knew it had to be his choice. Sometimes as I walked through the evening streets, looking into brightly-lit windows, I felt overwhelmingly that 'home' was elsewhere, unattainable.

CHAPTER 3

We had to wait almost an hour at the hospital for the death certificate to be issued while Michael's body lay there on the bed behind the curtains, or maybe was even already on its way to the morgue. The nursing sister who had stayed with us finally clocked off and went home, handing us over to a sweet young Irish nurse we had not previously met. We couldn't bear hanging around in the gloomy relatives' room so went down to the café in the basement in search of some dinner, but all they had left was some dried-up lasagne that stuck in our throats.

Finally we were able to leave, and took a taxi back to the friend's house where Ruairi was staying. I wanted to tell him properly about Michael's death. My friend had lit a fire for us and we cuddled on the hearthrug together, while I explained what had happened; I don't think either of us cried at this stage – we had both known what was coming. Besides, it all seemed completely unreal, even to me, and I had been there in person, unlike Ruairi who had last seen his dad in hospital the day before, an inert figure with tubes sticking out of him. Until quite recent times children were kept away from death and in some cases not even properly told about it – 'Daddy's gone away' or 'gone to sleep'. They were certainly not expected to attend funerals, even those of a parent. Things have changed, and it is now understood that bereaved children fare better if they are given a chance to experience and understand what is happening; but there are limits, and I think watching your father's breathing tube being removed is beyond them.

My friend insisted we should stay the night, which was a great relief. I'd have to go home at some point, but the thought of walking into our dark, empty house at that time of night was daunting. We were utterly exhausted, but nonetheless, after the children had gone to bed, my sister, my friend and I stayed up late into the night talking by firelight. I wondered whether I'd ever be able to sleep again, but when I got into bed that night I slept deeply and properly for the first time that week, and woke feeling calm and clear. Many bereaved people speak of waking in the morning with a vague sense of something amiss and then experiencing anew the devastating shock of loss, but this didn't really happen to me; from the beginning I awoke to a feeling of complete clarity. I was to learn that acceptance of death didn't mean you could avoid the pain of bereavement, but that would come later. For the moment I was still on something of a strange high.

Although it was Friday, Ruairi didn't go to school. One of Michael's friends came to drive us back to the house and as we walked in through the front door, I tried to imagine that we were bringing Michael home with us, in spirit if not in body. It had been our home together for ten years, and he was embedded in the very dust of the place, in particular his study which almost never got cleaned. At first I had to keep reminding myself that he was not simply out somewhere, or away for work, and would be back later.

One of the first things I did that day was throw out a few pieces of Michael's clothing that I had long detested: his tatty old dressing-gown full of holes; a badly worn-down pair of boots. I simply dropped them in the bin as if taking advantage of his absence to clean up his life for him. I have known a few widows who choose to pack up and dispose of all their partner's clothes the day after their death, though many others still keep the slippers under the bed and the coat on the door for years. Perhaps it is easier to deal with someone's belongings in the early days than later on; as time goes by the things that a dead person has touched take on the power of forensic evidence that they existed. I lived with black bags of Michael's clothes piled in the corner of our bedroom for several months before I could bring myself to get rid of them. Eventually I donated some to a local street-drinkers' project, wondering if one day I might see someone slumped over a beer on a park bench and mistake him for Michael. I took the rest to a charity shop; walking away I had to suppress an urge to rush straight in and buy them all back.

Bizarrely, my predominant feeling at first was relief, though from what I'm not sure: maybe for getting to the end of an awful week, or maybe the guilty relief of the survivor. Maybe – and I'm sure Ruairi felt this also – we knew Michael was now 'safe' and we didn't need to worry about him any more. His anxiety had been an almost physical force in our daily lives, and it was as though someone had suddenly flicked a switch and turned it off. I don't think that I have ever been such a consistently calm and tolerant parent as I was in those weeks: a 'Stepford mum', a friend called it, predicting that it would not and could not last.

At any rate we were not alone much of the time. There's a tremendous energy around death – an excited buzz that draws people in. I wonder if it could be something physical, someone's life force released into the world and needing to find an outlet; scientists now say that energy never disappears but just transforms itself into another form. Of course, it's a particular drama when a young person dies, because it's more unusual and therefore considered tragic. The death of another also reminds us, inevitably, of the transience of our own life and its precious brevity.

There was a palpable sense of shock and distress at Michael's death amongst those who had known him in the poetry and music worlds. From the moment I got home from the hospital

I was fielding phone calls and opening piles of letters and cards: far too many to think of replying to them. I got used to receiving large deliveries of post every day and was rather dismayed when it eventually tailed off. Friends and colleagues wrote, of course, but also many people who had only been readers of Michael's poems, or perhaps met him once, at a workshop or reading. They spoke of his charm and talent, how kind and encouraging he'd been to them personally, how his presence lit up the room. 'A thoroughly splendid fellow!' was how one of them described him.

Some of the phone calls, from distraught friends or even just admirers of Michael, went something like: 'I don't know how you're coping with this because I . . . *sob!!*' Of course it is important and reassuring to know that your loved one mattered to others, that others are grieving too; but for a while I felt completely swamped in other people's distress, which made it almost impossible to know what my own feelings were. In the first days I asked friends who were there to answer the phone for me and make sure nobody turned up at the house uninvited, and I delegated calls spreading the news to other people.

It sounds stupid, but I don't think I had realised until then how well known Michael was; after all, poetry is the Cinderella of the arts, down in the kitchen sweeping the ashes while others attend the glittering ball. Michael didn't have the public profile of some of his contemporaries; his reputation was mainly amongst other poets. However, rather like Charles Dickens, he was a consummate performer of his own work and won admiration through his personal appearances around the country. It hadn't even occurred to me that there would be obituaries but of course writers love to write about each other, and there were articles in most of the broadsheets. Pages were set up on the internet where people could add their own comments – in addition to many genuine tributes, this inevitably attracted what a friend called 'the brass section', keen to trumpet their personal connection with the great man. To my abiding shame one of Michael's aunts only learned of his death through an article in the *Evening Standard,* as I had not yet rung her, meaning to wait until the funeral date was confirmed.

A friend suggested I take photos of his study, a big room at the front of the house with shelves of books lining every wall. I had to work in collage to take it all in: the desk and the cluttered mantelpiece full of animal skulls, feathers, photographs and assorted memorabilia. Although very dusty, the room was unusually and mysteriously tidy. Earlier in the summer I had offered to spend a day helping Michael sort out his papers, which had got into their usual state of chaos. The process always resembled an archaeological dig: attempting to salvage anything important from the mounds of stuff piled on the desk and floor, while prising unread *Times Literary Supplements* out of his grip and putting them into the recycling. (Once, when a flat we lived in was broken into, the police exclaimed at the state of Michael's study, which they assumed had been ransacked by the burglars. We had to explain that it always looked like this – impossible to tell if anything had been taken, and, yes, that was his credit card on the floor, which was where he kept it. Michael claimed that his motto was: 'A thing for every place and every place with a thing in it.') But now everything, even the insides of the desk drawers, was neatly arranged, as though he had been secretly putting his affairs in order without any help from me.

Thinking about the last year of his life, I realised that he had recently tied up a lot of other loose ends, as though subconsciously preparing himself for what was to come. In the past months he had reconnected with several old friends whom he had not seen for a long time, including a fellow band member from long ago in Chicago who he had lost touch with, and a reunion with his sister in New York after several years virtually out of contact. We had also spent time together clearing out a room in the house where I would set up my Alexander practice, and disposing of a lot of stuff in the process – it had seemed at the time like an exhumation of the past.

There were even stranger things. Just a few weeks earlier, I had asked Michael to download a song from the internet, which I had heard and liked. The song, 'Sand and Water' by Beth Chapman, was written after the death of her husband, and, although it wasn't really his style of music, Michael commented that it was rather moving. Listening to it now, I realised with a shock that in the second verse of the song she talks about the son they had together, who she would now be raising alone; she seemed to be telling my own story. On the lighter side, a friend told me that Michael and she had been discussing a project he was working on with a composer which centred on ideas of mortality – apparently her last words to him had been something like 'Good luck with death!'

We had to go and register his death at Camden Registry Office where it struck me that only seventeen months previously I had stood in a similar office in Haringey to get married. Michael and I were together for twenty-one years but only married very late in the day, thanks largely to his change of heart after becoming a father. Now I was heartily glad that we had been married. For one thing, I learned I would be entitled to bereavement benefits, which you do not get unless legally wed, and it simplified the whole process of dealing with his death. In any case, I felt Michael had truly been my husband and I had earned the title of 'widow'. I have since become an advocate for marriage, especially when there are children in a relationship – people simply do not realise how little protection and legal entitlement you have in this country if you do not formalise the arrangement.

The next step was to organise the funeral. Because we have largely lost the ceremonial of organised religion, there is a fashion these days for organising your own funeral in advance, but this seems hubristic to me. Funerals are for the living, not for the dead. Of course, if you loved someone you might very well want to carry out their last wishes and give them a suitable send-off. But, beyond expressing a preference for cremation or burial, I don't see that we have any place trying to keep hold of the reins of control beyond our earthly existence. In planning Michael's funeral I thought carefully about what we – the mourners – needed to remember him by, to conjure his life. But I have no idea whether it's 'what he would have wanted', other than a couple of favourite songs he had mentioned and the general sense that he had been adored and would be missed.

When my father died I felt very excluded from the process. While nominally put in charge of organising the music for the funeral, I was not allowed to play what I really wanted: the trad jazz that I always associated with my dad and to which he remained loyal his whole life. A friend of his who died young had been buried in full New Orleans style with a marching band, but there was no question of my even playing a record; my mother said she didn't think it 'seemly', and my sister, who took charge of the arrangements, backed her up for a quiet life. The crematorium service, although personalised to an extent, didn't seem to have anything of my relationship to my father in it, and it wasn't until we sprinkled his ashes into a nearby river months later – he always loved the water and messing about in boats – that I felt I had done him justice and could mourn properly.

But Michael's funeral was all mine to organise and I realised at once that I would need to keep it small, otherwise it would rapidly become unmanageable, given the number of people clearly touched by his death. I decided it would be better to have a larger memorial event later on, and to invite only his closest friends and family, and mine, to the actual funeral. One musician who had played with Michael very occasionally over the years was furious at not being allowed to attend – he implied that I wanted to keep Michael all to myself and was denying him the right to mourn. I suggested instead that he could visit the funeral home.

I had already researched alternative funerals on the internet and found a local funeral director who specialised in 'ecological' funerals, called 'Green Endings'. Michael was a city boy to the core and in no way an environmentalist – he could barely be persuaded to sort the rubbish for recycling – so I wasn't going to condemn him to eternity under a tree. However, I thought they might be open to something more personal than the bland off-the-peg crematorium ceremony that most of my relatives seemed to end up with. The funeral director was a marvellous South African woman around my age with dramatic long white hair. She told us we could do whatever we liked with our allotted forty-minute slot at the crematorium, and together she and I concocted a programme of music, poetry and a short candle-lighting ceremony.

Although I could have run everything myself, she recommended engaging a celebrant of some sort to hold it all together. Michael had been brought up Catholic but had well and truly lapsed, so a priest was out of the question: however, I had been to a humanist funeral a year before and found that for me it lacked a sense of the transcendent. I wanted to find a way of bringing a spiritual element to the ceremony without having a religious service, which would also be inappropriate for most of Michael's friends.

The funeral director put me in touch with a private celebrant who came over to spend a couple of hours with me talking about Michael. She was happy to work in whatever way I wanted and we decided to include the section on death from Kahlil Gibran's *The Prophet*, which speaks of death as the ultimate freedom: 'And when the earth has claimed your limbs, then can you truly dance.' It is always strange to have someone who didn't know the dead person speak about them at a funeral, but she did it so convincingly that several people assumed she was a family friend. She suggested we could have a point in the ceremony where mourners might be invited to speak informally about

Michael; in the event only one person spoke up, but this may have been because I deliberately didn't announce it in advance, fearing that certain people might hog the floor.

My memory of this time is of a constant bustle and busyness – people to see, places to be, things to organise and no time to think about sadness or mourning. Friends came most evenings to cook dinner, sometimes with their children, and I had a sense for perhaps the first time in my life of being held by community, of having people I could rely on in a very practical way if I needed them. I remember thinking that I needed to learn how to ask for help more often, because people were clearly so willing. But this level of support and interest only lasted a short time; it would not be long before everyone's attention inevitably returned to their own busy lives.

It was the same with the many people I knew less well who were drawn to me after Michael's death. Suddenly everyone wanted to talk to me, to know how it felt, and I was happy to tell them. I suppose I quite enjoyed being the centre of attention. But I quite often had the experience of thinking that I had become much closer to someone, only to have them almost ignore me when next we met. They had got what they needed and moved on. But I was still in the thick of it.

My closest friend offered to host the funeral party at her house, and I gave her a pile of photographs of Michael to create a memorial display. We put out a beautiful notebook with marbled covers that we had bought on our honeymoon in Venice, for people to autograph. A couple of women friends who weren't coming to the funeral helped prepare lunch, and another friend organised flowers, bright orange gerberas, for the coffin and to decorate the crematorium.

I had asked for no floral tributes, because they always seem such a terrible waste to me, piled briefly outside the crematorium and then left to rot, like the sea of cellophane-wrapped ones abandoned outside Princess Diana's Kensington Palace. Besides,

Michael could hardly be said to have loved flowers; he once bought me, reduced for quick sale at the supermarket, a single sprig of white gypsophila which I meanly told him was like giving someone the parsley garnish without the meal. Other than that I don't remember ever getting flowers from him.

Despite my request, many bouquets were sent to me at home, including several large arrangements of lilies that would have looked better in a funeral parlour. I quickly ran out of vases and places to put them and began to feel oppressed by the florist-shop atmosphere. Flowers require looking after – they run out of water, drop petals and leaves, need rearranging. To this day mixed floral bouquets tend to evoke funerals, and if I ever buy flowers for myself, it is something simple like a bunch of daffodils. Although sending flowers seems to be what immediately comes to mind when people hear of a death, birth or other crisis, there are other options such as chocolate, alcohol, or even food! There used to be, and probably still is in many parts of the world, a custom of friends and neighbours leaving ready-cooked dishes on the doorstep of bereaved families. I certainly appreciated any offers to feed us and the Sainsbury's vouchers sent by my fellow students from the Alexander Technique College were an inspired choice.

I wondered aloud if I should choose a charity for people to donate to, instead of sending flowers – one for struggling poets, perhaps – and someone suggested that Ruairi should be the beneficiary. I was doubtful at first: it seemed somehow to be taking advantage, but of course people would have a choice whether they wished to contribute. So we set up a fund for Ruairi and donations came in thick and fast from people all over the country and even from America. The funeral director had offered to administer the fund initially and was as amazed as we were at the generous response from Michael's friends and fans. Later the Poetry Society took over as collecting point, and money continued to come in for over a year, with poets donating their reading fees and organising fund-raising events. In addition, the Royal Literary Fund got in touch with me to ask if we needed help, and within two months they had organised a substantial grant to keep us afloat.

A colleague of Michael's offered to call and cancel all Michael's upcoming engagements and teaching commitments; I was painfully aware that this meant there would be no further income, and of course he didn't have a pension. I had only just finished my Alexander Technique training that summer and had no clients yet; I was earning nothing at this point, and we had only small savings. So this generous support from the poetry community was literally a life-saver. That and the offer from a wealthy friend to pay the £2000-plus funeral expenses and fund the memorial; I had not realised how expensive dying was.

A couple of Michael's close friends who had not been able to get to the hospital in time asked to see him in the funeral parlour, which meant he would have to be prepared for viewing. I felt I had already said goodbye and didn't think anything would be served by taking Ruairi to see his father's body, but I understood their need to visit him. I picked out a bright red shirt that Michael loved to wear, though it rather clashed with his skin colour, and some plain black trousers of which he owned several identical pairs from Marks and Spencer, in varying sizes to accord with his shifting waistline. When my dad died we had a problem finding decent underwear and socks: all of his looked too old and wretched but somehow it seemed pointless to buy new clothes just to have them cremated. Luckily Michael had some relatively decent underwear, but his socks were a motley collection full of holes, so I donated a pair of my own.

As I write this, it is as though I remember dressing him for the final journey – smoothing the collar, tucking in the shirt-tails. But of course all this was done by the funeral director in the back of her shop; I simply brought everything to her in a carrier bag. I had wanted to send my father off with a bag of his favourite Liquorice Allsorts in his pocket, like the Ancient Egyptians who were buried with all they might need for the next world, but I had been too embarrassed. For Michael, however, we chose several mementos to put in the coffin with him: Ruairi put in a drawing he had done that week, a little stuffed-toy Eskimo, and one of his baby teeth, which had actually fallen out in the hospital while he was visiting Michael – they often seemed to choose significant moments to pop out. I didn't know what to put in that could possibly represent the enormity of our years together, so I made a small heart out of birch twigs bound with red ribbon to tuck into his pocket.

From the plethora of 'green' alternatives – wicker, papier mâché, even cloth shrouds – I had chosen for Michael a plain pine coffin that looked as if it could have come flat-packed from Ikea. I amused myself thinking of funny Swedish-sounding names for it: 'Kofinn', 'Tod'. I have since read that for cremation purposes, wood is 'greener' than lighter substances, as it generates its own heat in the burning. On the day of the funeral, yet another beautiful bright sunny day, the funeral director drove the coffin to the crematorium in the back of her cream Mercedes estate, while we arrived separately in our own cars. As we pulled in to the cemetery gates we were brought to a crawl by a huge tailback of shiny black limousines loaded with monstrous floral tributes and overdressed mourners; the funeral ahead of ours was running late. We followed this cavalcade along the winding pathways to the crematorium at the far end of the cemetery, feeling distinctly like poor relations.

When we got married, just the year before, I had asked one of Michael's friends to drive us to the registry office, thinking he had a pretty decent car. To my surprise he arrived in a very disreputable-looking old vehicle on which Michael drew in the dirt on the back windscreen: 'MD ♥ MP'. We got stuck in a traffic jam en route and were pulled over by the police because the car's road tax had expired; luckily they realised (from the bouquet of flowers I was clutching?) that we were on our way to a special occasion and let us go with just a warning. We arrived at the registry office late and rather flustered, but luckily ours was the only ceremony scheduled that morning.

Now, seventeen months later, we gathered outside the crematorium, waiting for the rest of our party to arrive while the strains of Whitney Houston's 'I Will Always Love You' seeped out through the closed doors. In a sort of production line, mourners from one funeral are ushered out through a rear door so that they don't get mixed up with the next group. When our turn came to go in, I handed over my own CD of music to the man behind the curtain – again reminiscent of our wedding – and we took our seats.

There were only two representatives of Michael's family: a cousin and an elderly aunt who lived in Slough. His sister hadn't come over from America, saying she had lost her passport. My mother, my sister and her husband and my cousin were there to represent our family, and about twenty other close friends. Our wedding had been tiny: only ten people including us, a decision which caused more difficulties at the time than I had anticipated. I wanted all the guests to be able to sit at one table, but that meant leaving out people who clearly felt they should be invited. This time I felt I had got the balance about right and everyone who really needed to be there, was.

Four of Michael's friends acted as pall-bearers, carrying the coffin into the room and lifting it up onto the dais while another played the guitar softly. For our wedding it had proved so difficult to choose a poem that we had finally declared it a poetry-free zone; Michael's poem 'The Present', which is a perfect marriage poem, had already been used by my sister and several of our friends and didn't feel special any more. But we could not send him off without his beloved poetry, so at the funeral I read Donne's 'The Good Morrow', which had been on our wedding shortlist, and Ruairi's godfather read 'Haunts', the poem Michael had written for Ruairi about his own future death. It begins 'Don't be afraid, old son, it's only me . . .'

The fiddle-player from Michael's Irish band in Chicago, who had been there on the day we first met, played a beautiful slow air that Michael used to play on the tin whistle. Another friend read her own eulogy and then we all went up to the front in turn and lit candles to the accompaniment of Ry Cooder's 'Always Lift Him Up and Never Knock Him Down', a song that more than anything summed up Michael's generosity of spirit towards his fellow human beings and their weaknesses. At the end I lifted Ruairi up to the coffin to say goodbye, and he kissed it. I don't think either of us felt really sad at this moment; it was more a kind of sweet melancholy combined for me with a sense of a job well done – both the funeral and my life with Michael.

I had asked to watch the actual cremation as there was always something disturbing to me about just walking away from the coffin or seeing it disappear on a conveyor belt – shades of the Dave Allen comedy shows I watched as a child, when something always went awry. I felt a strong need to see the process through to the end: it's not something we commonly do any more, except in burials, but in other cultures the witnessing of that final moment is an essential part of the funeral rites. I had seen Hindu funerals in Varanasi, the holy city of India, where the body is carried through the crowded streets wrapped only in a shroud and then burned on an open pyre. In this country you can't actually see the coffin go up in flames, as the oven is too hot, but we were allowed to watch as it was slid on a trolley into the fiery red hole and the flames licked up around it. Just before they slammed the door shut I clutched my friend's arm: 'He's igniting!'

Then we returned to my friend's house for the lovely party she had organised. As at most of these events, much wine was consumed and everybody who had given up smoking had a few cigarettes just for the occasion. The lunch was magnificent, including a baked salmon and a gin-and-tonic jelly. As often at a wake, it had an initial atmosphere of jolly festivity rather than mourning, but later that evening, sitting with a group of my closest women friends after most of the guests had left, and listening to a CD of songs by the McGarrigle sisters, I was finally able to cry a little. I've always found it hard to cry at appropriate moments, perhaps from self-consciousness, or from a feeling that nothing is actually that emotionally straightforward. Or perhaps I was still just numb.

People expect you to react in a certain way to certain events and are baffled and even sometimes put out when you don't. But the emotions surrounding a death are so complex and changeable that simple sadness doesn't even begin to express it. When someone dies in a film or television drama, the loved ones always break down and sob loudly or become hysterical, but I think it is just as likely that they would sit in stunned silence. I would cry plenty over the coming years, but at this point I made a vow to myself, the quotation from *Hamlet* that my mother had written in my first autograph book when I was ten: 'This above all, to thine own self be true'.

CHAPTER 4

Two old friends stayed the night of the funeral with me, and the next day we took our children out to the park, as though everything were normal. One of them – herself a single parent – commented that I was going to have to give Ruairi a lot more attention from now on, and suddenly it hit me that I was now a lone parent. Ruairi had been going off to school as usual that week, taken and collected by other people, and friends had come round every evening, so I had barely had a chance to be alone with him. But there was no escaping the fact that we had only each other from now on. I had always felt huge regret at the passing of each fleeting phase of Ruairi's childhood, but now I felt ready, almost eager, for him to grow up.

In a sort of inner 'balloon debate', I found myself thinking that if one of us had to die, it was better that it had been Michael. How would he ever have coped with bringing up Ruairi on his own, when he could barely keep his own life together? Of course, he would probably have been scooped up pretty quickly by another woman; they always seemed to be hovering in the wings, ready to come running and tie his shoelaces, which he always left trailing. A poet as partner can be a very appealing prospect until you actually have to live with them. And it doesn't bear thinking about how as a couple we might have survived the death of Ruairi, though many people do have to face the awful tragedy of losing children.

We had sometimes dubbed our little family the 'Three Musketeers', hugging each other and declaring: 'All for one and one for all!' That night Ruairi and I tried out: 'Each for both and both for each!' but it didn't quite work, so a favourite teddy stood in for Michael; a tripod is a much more stable base. During those first weeks the sense of our isolation really hit me while waiting at the bus stop in the mornings to take Ruairi to school. I pictured a camera panning away from us, leaving two tiny figures clutching each other's hand in the middle of an enormous world. Who would keep the bears away? Marriage provides a layer of protection from the outside world that you are barely conscious of; now I felt raw, exposed, vulnerable, almost as though a layer of skin had been torn off my body.

Grief is a physically overwhelming experience and can be utterly exhausting. I was surprised to find that the physical sensation of losing Michael was very different from when my father died. Then it had felt as if a rock I didn't know I was standing on had been pulled away and the bottom had dropped out of my world: a constant sinking sensation in my belly, like going down too fast in a lift. But the pain of losing Michael seemed located around my chest and solar plexus: on occasion it was as sharp and winding as if I'd been stabbed, at other times a kind of pulling, empty feeling as though my centre had been ripped out.

A couple of days after the funeral I was lying in bed trying to make myself think about the future. What would I do now, what would become of us? I needed to make plans! Then I realised that the previous week I had had a whole other set of plans, and look what had happened to them – as the old saying goes: 'Make God laugh . . .' I was swamped by a wave of fear that took me into a mental free-fall, spiralling down through the void with no knowing where it would end. But suddenly on my way down this rabbit hole a thought came to me: 'What an adventure!' Freed from the path I had shared with Michael for twenty-one years, I had a whole voyage of discovery ahead of me.

The year before, a friend of ours had died after years battling breast cancer. She had been terrified of heights all her life, unable even to go up tall buildings, until one year while in remission from her illness and living in Brazil, where she had grown up, she decided to learn paragliding in order to try and conquer her fear. During her last months of life we sat and watched a video of her leaping into the air from a high cliff, shrieking with terror and exhilaration, and this image came back to me now. She had faced her death and separation from her young daughter with the same kind of courage; surely I could find the courage to live.

But we can't help but think about the future; it's one of the things that make us human, even though looking ahead is as much fantasy as, in its own way, is dwelling on the past. Around this time I had several clear insights, so strong they seemed almost like premonitions about my future life, or at least beacons of possibility. I could make my own choices now.

There was the question of where to live. When Michael first came to London from America we considered moving somewhere else altogether, somewhere more 'neutral', but it was clear that it would have to be a city: Edinburgh maybe, or Galway in Ireland. Michael had grown up in the Bronx and had lived only in Manhattan and Chicago; he was urban to his bones and always claimed that trees made him nervous. (Many people found this a surprising trait in a poet, believing that all poets, like Wordsworth, must have a profound affinity with nature.) But as his career became more established, London was clearly the best place for him to be, and I had resigned myself to living here into our old age. Now he was gone I had the freedom to live where *I* wanted – in the countryside, by the sea, even abroad. I could have a cottage down a lane with dogs and chickens, if I so desired. The sense of freedom was dizzying.

I also knew with certainty that I would one day have another partner, a whole second chapter of life; after all, I was only forty-six and had no intention of spending the rest of my days alone. I promised myself that it would be a different kind of relationship, more balanced and separate, a grown-up relationship in which I might be able to behave in a grown-up way. John Bayley, Iris Murdoch's husband, described their marriage as being like 'two animals in a field', and this image of two souls living peacefully alongside each other is immensely appealing. The poet Rilke says: 'I hold this to be the highest task for a bond between two people: that each protects the solitude of the other.'

I'm not sure how I'd manage it in purely practical terms as I rather like things my own way (and I gather the Bayley-Murdoch household arrangements were in truth rather chaotic), but emotionally I'd say there is a strong case for trying to stay out of each other's heads. When you meet your partner relatively young in life it is hard for the relationship to evolve out of its early dynamics, which are so much influenced by unmet childhood needs and old family patterns. But as you grow older you become more 'formed' as a person, so the chances are that it would be easier to retain boundaries in relationship to others. I didn't think I would ever again be swallowed up in love as I had been with Michael – I had had a soulmate, now I needed an earthly companion.

But who was I, what were my needs and priorities? I had always painted, written, composed music, but in our marriage it was clear who was the real artist and who the amanuensis. Michael was a hugely gifted writer, and poetry was clearly a vocation for him; I believed utterly in his talent and did my best to support his work. But this meant he was always the rose and I the gardener. Or, as a feminist slogan puts it, in front of every great woman is a man. It is very tempting as a woman, and particularly also a mother, to take second place to a partner's ambition, and of course there is a deal of reflected glory to be had by association with someone successful. It was too easy for me, dilettante that I can be, to take my own creativity less seriously and treat it as a mere diversion, although I have always known that giving expression to this side of things is fundamental to the health of my soul. Perhaps now it was my turn to be the artist, if I dared.

The first signs that my support network was running out of steam came the Monday after the funeral, when it was time to start tackling the paperwork, of which there is an astonishing amount after a death. Many people just hand it all over to a solicitor, but our financial affairs were relatively simple and as I was the one who had been in charge of them anyway (as with everything else practical in our lives) I decided to handle the probate myself. I knew what needed to be done, but the emotional effort required to begin the task was daunting and I longed for someone to stand beside me and give me courage to get started.

I rang a practical-minded friend who had helped arrange the funeral, but she said she had too much else to do that day – a perfectly reasonable response, but one that in my vulnerability felt like a door being slammed in my face. If you are someone who finds it hard to ask for help, any small refusal makes it doubly difficult to ask again. It began to sink in that this was one of a long list of things I would have to tackle alone.

I started working through the necessary phone calls at a rate of about one a day – each one leaving me bruised and tearful. In a society where we pretend for the most part that death doesn't happen, I frequently felt as though I were the first person ever to be bereaved, and the confused and unsympathetic reactions of front-line staff were startling. I would begin by explaining that my husband had died the week before and I needed to find out how to proceed, to which the most common reply was an embarrassed 'Oh!' I felt I was just an annoying problem to be dealt with; there was no acknowledgement of the news I had just imparted, no simple human 'I'm sorry'. One bank employee told me she could only discuss matters with the account holder – 'Who, I have just told you, is dead!' I shouted.

Another operator quoted from a prepared script, telling me that the building society 'extended its condolences to me in my loss' – somewhat stilted but better than nothing.

One afternoon I managed to get myself and Ruairi out to the bank with all the correct paperwork, as instructed on the phone, to close Michael's account. The young woman behind the counter, on hearing my request, asked peevishly: 'What do you want *me* to do?' I explained that I had never dealt with a death before and I rather thought she should be telling me how to proceed. I then had to wait to see a 'customer care' operative, who told me she didn't usually work at this branch, and could I come back tomorrow to see someone else? At this point I broke down – how little they understood the huge effort it had taken me to get there that day. I sometimes wish bereaved people could wear black armbands as in Victorian times, to indicate that although they may look normal they are barely functioning, and need careful and gentle handling. In the event she took in the paperwork, promising to forward it to the right department, and it was promptly lost. The whole process had to be repeated two weeks later.

The only people who seemed to have a clue how to behave were the Probate Department, who explained everything I needed to know in a clear and sympathetic way unexpected from a dry legal institution, and the lovely Glaswegian ladies in the Bereavement Benefits office, who clearly knew how to respond with sympathy; unfortunately that service has since been reorganised and those kind motherly women are no longer the ones you speak to. There should really be a sort of 'one-stop shop' for bereavement, where a care worker will make all the calls on your behalf and take you through the long list of organisations who need to be informed, each of which seems to require a different combination of paperwork. Solicitors charge a huge fee for this largely administrative service, and my guess is you'd end up chasing them anyway. Also, having these kind of things to do does in some way help you keep going in the first weeks of bereavement; it seems purposeful and finite, unlike the great journey of grief that awaits.

The Deed of Probate was granted within a couple of months; I had to go for an interview at Somerset House, which was rather daunting but turned out to be a formality. Then copies of the Deed of Probate had to be sent to everyone concerned before they would release any money to me. I was lucky that I had my family to help me out during this period, and at least had a little money in my own bank account. I'm not sure how people manage when this process drags on for ages, sometimes years, with financial assets frozen. At least we had made proper wills when Ruairi was born, because simply being married does not guarantee that you automatically receive your spouse's legacy – it can end up being divided amongst other relatives, and it's not unknown for widowed people to lose their home. We spend so much time avoiding the thought of death that many of us meet it quite unprepared, even in the most practical of matters.

Bereavement benefits, which I had never even heard of before Michael's death, were more complicated to arrange. Michael had not paid a full quota of National Insurance contributions, having arrived in this country only at the age of thirty, and subsequently worked in a number of part-time jobs. Some of it was our fault – we could have spotted the gaps and paid up voluntarily, but we didn't think it very important at the time. I wondered if I could back-pay some of his contributions to increase my entitlement, but the National Insurance rules are among the most complicated and arcane in existence, and the staff on the helplines don't understand them either. Fortunately a friend who works in welfare rights was able to photocopy the relevant piece of the law for me, which I posted to the authorities concerned, and they allowed me to make up a few years' payments. I would receive approximately half the

Widowed Parent's Allowance until Ruairi turned eighteen, plus an immediate one-off payment towards funeral expenses.

For the first time in a couple of weeks I felt brave enough to go and pick Ruairi up from school myself, as he had thus far been taken and collected by friends. I took my usual route, making a right turn onto a side street only to find this turn had recently been made illegal. I was immediately pulled over by police – I had not noticed the new signs. When I explained that this was the first time I had driven that way since my husband's death (trying hard not to cry in case I was thought manipulative), the policeman took pity on me and 'issued' me a blank piece of paper instead of a ticket, saying he had to make it look like he was doing his job. Little moments of human kindness like this are what sustain you.

It's so hard to walk into a place where everyone knows your story but no one quite knows what to say. I was worried that I'd either be overwhelmed by people wanting to console me, or, as has happened to many people I know, be greeted with silence. I have found over the years that even the best-meaning people simply don't have the words to express their feelings about bereavement, and this can cause them to say rather odd and sometimes hurtful things, or nothing at all, which is even stranger. I needn't have worried, though – my friends at the school welcomed me back gently and warmly, and had clearly been waiting for the chance to enfold me in the community again. A few weeks later they presented me with a colourful wool blanket, each square knitted by a mother in Ruairi's class and bound together by a crocheted edge. It was an amazing gesture of warmth and holding.

Michael was of course a familiar figure to them, on the school run and occasionally attending parents' events, but I was much more involved in the school and so their grieving was mostly for me and Ruairi. His class teacher held a little ceremony for the children, where they lit a candle, looked at photos and said what they remembered about Michael. A couple of Ruairi's close friends who knew Michael well were very upset, and of course no child wants to hear that a parent can die suddenly. A few weeks later while accompanying a school outing I overheard one little girl asking Ruairi: 'What's it like, not having a dad?', to which he breezily replied 'Fine!' More than anything Ruairi just wanted to be normal, to fit in, not to be the boy who was marked out by his father dying.

But of course nothing was normal. Everyone kept telling me how strong I was and how well I was coping, and it's true – I *was* strong, I *was* coping, and I was still mostly held in the bubble of calm and purposefulness that had encircled Michael's death. I was also deeply traumatised, so much so that it took about a year for me to begin to realise the extent of it. In the first weeks the main signs were a sort of flustered confusion that made me forget to eat, brush my hair, take baths – as though my physical needs were slipping under the radar. It was not unlike the first weeks of parenthood, when you are so immersed in the new baby's needs that you don't even manage to get dressed until mid-afternoon.

Nights were the worst time. That moment at the end of the day when you are all alone, the house is quiet and there is nothing left to do except go to bed, seemed unbearably bleak and lonely. I have always had insomniac tendencies and now my sleep became completely erratic. I got sleeping pills from the doctor, but they made me feel rotten and hung-over in the mornings, so usually I would pad around the house in the dark for several hours, then nap in the daytime after Ruairi had gone to school. My favourite comforter at any time of day or night was a cup of hot chocolate laced with whisky. Tears came more easily in the depth of night; once, completely distraught, I rang my sister at 3 a.m., just to hear a familiar voice. 'I can't stop crying!' I told her.

Sleep has always been something of an elusive wonder to me. I so envy people who drop off as soon as they get into bed, as

I frequently lie awake despite being exhausted: novelist Barbara Kingsolver describes this as 'you close the fridge door but the light stays on'. Or I might be almost or even completely asleep and suddenly click wide awake again for no obvious reason, sometimes after only a few minutes, then be unable to find my way back into sleep. Apparently I didn't sleep well as a baby either, standing up in my cot and 'burbling' all night, as my mother put it. Perhaps I was on the alert even then; certainly, since Ruairi was a baby I have never slept right through the night and am easily disturbed by the slightest sound. Or I wake much too early, whereupon anxious thoughts immediately crowd in. At times I wondered with desperation whether I would ever again get enough rest.

When people asked: 'How are you?' I didn't know how to reply; like Ruairi, part of me wanted to say: 'Fine!', but I knew I wasn't. What I often said was that if they asked me in six months' time I might be able to tell them how I had felt at that moment, because it was actually all rather a blur. But a blur it remained – those first few months are hard to recall. They had that weird, time-distorting quality of seeming to grind slowly by while at the same time passing in the blink of an eye. The emotions of bereavement are so complex: spiralling down into your past so that you relive all your life's experience of loss; tearing you remorselessly apart so that you are forced to rebuild yourself almost from scratch; changing from moment to moment in a single day. I had hardly even begun yet.

One thing that confused me was that I didn't really seem to miss Michael. But when someone has just died, you have seen them very recently, so it feels more like they are just away some-where and will soon be back. It is only as the weeks and months go on that it begins to dawn that this separation is permanent. Even so, if someone has been a big part of your daily life it is a long time – years even – before you stop expecting them to walk in the door. Katherine Whitehorn, writing in *The Guardian* of losing her husband after forty years, describes marriage as the water you swim in, the air you breathe, without even being aware of it. Widowhood, she says, is like having to 'learn to live in another country in which you're an unwilling refugee'.

In some ways it gets harder and harder to comprehend the reality of someone's death with the passing of time. At the beginning it all seemed brutally clear – I had watched Michael die before my eyes, and I knew he would not come back. But not all parts of my brain were in on the secret; I often found myself telling someone about his death while some other part of my brain was saying 'What?! What do you mean?', as though hearing the shocking news for the first time. The truth is that we cannot understand death from within life – it is quite literally unimaginable. Someone who was a huge presence on earth has gone, but where? Surely not far away – I felt as though Michael had taken up residence in my head, in my thoughts. He felt closer to me in some ways than when alive.

I returned to the National Neurological Hospital for a debriefing meeting: something offered to all relatives of people who die there. They should have told me to wait at reception, but instead I made my way on auto-pilot upstairs to the ward where Michael had died. As I got out of the lift I almost passed out, hit by a wave of emotions and visceral memories; I was rescued by a nurse and taken to an office on another floor. The progress of the meeting was rather hampered by the fact that Michael's notes had gone missing, something that would be a feature of all attempts to investigate his death. My main concern was to find out how Ruairi might be affected – could he be at risk in the future because of the family history? A friend's daughter had died of a brain haemorrhage, aged thirteen, some years before, but the doctors reassured me that the causes for it happening in a child were different from those in an adult.

They were unable to tell me what had caused Michael's haemorrhage. There had not been a post-mortem, because once the brain is flooded with blood, it is impossible to tell what started it – I was told it could have been a ruptured aneurysm, or something called AVM, a malformation of veins and arteries that sends blood the wrong way, or just a weak spot. Brain-imaging techniques will undoubtedly become much more sophisticated in the future, but would I be able to suggest to Ruairi that he have scans done at some stage without making him feel that he was living under the axe? A friend who has had several close relatives die of motor neurone disease chooses not to have the tests which might determine his own likelihood of developing it – there is as yet no cure, and he simply does not want to know. It can also adversely affect things like insurance and getting a mortgage. Michael had always been haunted by the fear of dying of a heart attack like his father, but it turned out that another fate awaited him. As Ruairi said, 'These Donaghys have a way of dying, don't they?'

A group of Michael's friends had thrown themselves into helping arrange a big memorial service – they, too, obviously felt better having something practical to do with their grief. We booked a beautiful, unusual building: the Union Chapel in Islington, an octagonal Victorian chapel which is also a venue for concerts. Michael and I had been to see Altan, one of our favourite Irish bands, play there ten years before, shortly before the flute player died of cancer. In addition to the chapel, which seated eight hundred, there was a large room upstairs with a bar, where we could party afterwards, and another room downstairs for dancing. We would send him off in style.

The memorial was like a much larger version of the funeral, this time attended by over five hundred people. Various friends spoke about Michael, read poems and played music – these elements are common to all such gatherings, but in Michael's case they reflected and honoured his life's work. There was even a recording of the man himself reading one of his own poems,

'The Hunter's Purse', after which someone played the Irish tune of that name on the flute.

A guitarist who had been in a band with Michael for many years was booked to sing 'The Lakes of Pontchartrain', the only song that Michael was able to get vaguely in tune, and which he had sung to me on a fire escape in Chicago our first summer together. But on the morning of the memorial the guitarist rang to say he would not be able to make it due to a 'plumbing emergency'. I later learned with no surprise that he was at another – paid – gig. I was angry for a while, but reminded myself that Michael would have understood and forgiven him straight away.

I thought hard about what my contribution might be, and decided that the question I was most likely to be asked by everyone was – what happened? I knew already that there were stories that Michael had had a heart attack, a brain tumour – the usual Chinese whispers. So I decided I would tell the story of his death, so that everyone would understand. In some ways this was pure self-protection, so that I didn't have to explain it to people one by one, but to my surprise it was considered by everyone there to be an enormously generous act. I stood before a huge audience, without any stage-fright for the first time in my life, because I knew everyone there wished me well, and spoke into an attentive silence.

To end the service, myself and a friend taught everyone a three-part traditional African song, the words of which mean 'Will we meet again in heaven?' After an initial shyness, the audience filled the chapel with their voices. Then all the children present, who had made a valiant attempt at sitting still in the front pew all afternoon, jiggled and danced to the anarchic Bonzo Dog Band's 'The Intro and the Outro', a track that Michael had said he would like at his funeral, in the idle way one has of discussing these things when death seems a long way off.

That evening there was a big party that lasted until midnight, with people spread out over the several floors of the old building. There was dancing, both 'set-dancing' to Irish music and getting down to James Brown, plenty of drinking (poets are big boozers), and even a fist fight: apparently a disagreement about avant-garde poetry, which would probably have gratified Michael. The children ran around under our feet, charging wildly up and down the stairs, and I wandered around feeling somewhere between a guest of honour and completely irrelevant, since everyone agreed who should really have been there. It is a cliché that only the good die young, but it does sometimes seem that it is the brightest stars who burn out the fastest. It's clear that with Michael many people had a sense of not knowing what they had until it was gone – both in terms of his huge talent and his huge heart.

'Our Life Stories'...

At long last Michael made the decision to come and live with me in London. As his father was from Northern Ireland, Michael was entitled to 'Right of Abode' in the UK, which I had helped him organise during a trip to America that year. We had to track down his parents' marriage certificate at a Bronx registry office, where after two attempts at guessing the right date we struck lucky; Michael was rather vague about his family history. When the time came for him to move, I stepped back from proceedings and he arranged the whole thing himself, shipping over a large number of boxes full of books and records and little else. It was an amazingly romantic gesture of commitment to our relationship, and must have been an enormous wrench for him to leave everything familiar behind.

But there were other things than me drawing him here. Having grown up with immigrant Irish parents who considered themselves in perpetual exile, this side of the Atlantic had always had an allure of 'home' about it for him. Also, he felt that his formal, erudite poetry was more suited to the British literary scene, which was confirmed when within a year he was taken up for publication by Oxford University Press. Michael delighted in the way poetry seemed much more a part of ordinary life here: British newspapers regularly printed poems, and poets were even sometimes mentioned on the news, whereas in America it was considered an élite specialism confined to the literary academy.

Music was also an essential ingredient for him – actually in some ways I think it was more fundamental to his sense of well-being than poetry. He often seemed to have something 'playing' in his head, his foot tapping to a secret melody. His Irish band in Chicago had more or less fallen apart by the time he left, but his arrival in London coincided with a huge and thriving traditional music scene, before the 'Celtic Tiger' economy sucked all the expatriate musicians home to Ireland. We could walk to a pub session most nights of the week from our Archway flat. I was by now playing the piano in a *popular all-women ceilidh band, the Sheelas, while he formed his own group, the Slip Jigolos, who played weekly in a Camden pub (they were all men, though nobody seemed to think this worthy of mention).*

Nonetheless it was a difficult period of adjustment for us, and, feeling in some way responsible for his happiness here, I put a lot of energy into trying to make things run smoothly and help him feel at home. Before he arrived, I had lined his room in our flat with egg boxes, to absorb the sound of his practising the tin whistle. On Michael's first day in London he rang me at work to say he felt like an escaped prisoner of war trying to evade capture: he had asked in a pub for 'a cup of tea to go' and in a typewriter shop for a machine 'without the V.A.T.' and been met with uncomprehending stares. Divided by a common language, as they say.

Growing up with my mother's mental volatility, I had learned to be constantly on the alert and to adapt my behaviour to her state of mind; her moods were the emotional weather of our family life. I transferred this model of relationship onto my life with Michael, taking on his inner life as my own. Sometimes I felt like a patch of pale watercolour being bled over by a large black ink blot, though this says as much about my own lack of emotional boundaries as about any desire on his part to overwhelm me. Despite our great love for each other, I often felt insecure in the relationship, and for years was anxious that he might decide to move back to America, even when it was clear that he was settled in the UK.

On his arrival in England Michael had been able to sign straight on the dole while I carried on working to pay our bills. Having volunteered at a Planned Parenthood clinic in Chicago, I had found a job at a women's health centre in London, initially as a receptionist but later counselling women seeking abortion. I marvel now that I thought I could offer advice from my twenty-six-year-old perspective, but I suppose I have always been a good listener and I have an abiding fascination with people's feelings and inner lives. Meanwhile I completed my Women's Studies MA and planned to develop my dissertation about feminism and infertility treatment into a book.

Michael was rapidly establishing a reputation here in the poetry world. His first book with Oxford University Press, Shibboleth, published in 1988, won the prestigious Whitbread Prize for poetry, and we were invited to a black-tie dinner at the brewery's London headquarters. My cousin later sent us a glamorous photograph of ourselves taken that evening, which she had come across in Hello! magazine – my first and last brush with celebrity. On the back of this success, Michael was offered plenty of readings and other work, and began teaching regular poetry evening classes for Birkbeck College and City University, which he would continue until his death.

Meanwhile I started giving piano lessons, ostensibly to support myself while working on my book. I had played the piano since the age of nine, but I now decided I'd better study for a teaching diploma, which meant practising the piano several hours a day. The book remained unfinished but I gained my diploma and over the next few years branched out into teaching music in a whole variety of settings, from running my own local parent-toddler music sessions to teaching in adult education at the City Lit, and supporting the music curriculum in local primary schools.

I was amazed by the number of people I came across who considered themselves 'tone deaf', most of whom just lacked confidence in their voices, having been told as children that they were unmusical. (If you are not good at maths they make you do extra, but if you struggle with music you are usually told to be quiet and not spoil it for everyone else.) I asked the City Lit if I could put on specialist classes for non-singers; they were reluctant but agreed to let me try. I had obviously hit a nerve, as the classes quickly became extremely successful and popular.

Due to difficulties with landlords we had to move several times in quick succession during our first years in London. On one of these occasions we decided to experiment with living apart for a while, which we had never done after the first brief summer. However, *my flat quickly became 'base camp' and Michael's a messy private retreat, which didn't seem fair; staying over with him felt too much like camping, something I had to brace myself for. Also, many of our friends assumed that we were splitting up, and several women made moves on Michael.*

I decided we should buy our own flat. Michael's father had, to his surprise, left him a little money, my parents helped us with the down payment, and we got a mortgage somehow despite our precarious incomes. (This was the property boom of the nineteen-eighties.) Michael, whose family had never owned their own home, feared we were living in bourgeois comfort beyond our means, but I was glad we had somewhere that was ours and wouldn't have to move again.

CHAPTER 5

After the memorial my protective bubble of calm and purposefulness began to evaporate. Once all the attention had died down, it came home forcefully to me that this was my life now, not just a brief drama of which, in some sense, I had been the star.

In *The Year of Magical Thinking* Joan Didion speaks about the way we unconsciously believe that once certain rituals are completed, certain milestones passed, everything will return to normal; deep inside we can't help but hope that if only we perform the ceremonies well enough, utter the right kind of spell, keep the shoes ready in the wardrobe, the dead person will return. The first years of grieving are full of reality checks: he's still dead, I'm still alone, can this truly be going on for ever?

A few nights after the memorial I dreamed about Michael for the first time. It turned out he had not been dead at all, but simply away for a while, and was coming home now. I was quite annoyed – I had publicly mourned him and felt I'd been made a fool of. I told him if he wanted to come back there'd have to be some major changes between us. When I woke up I felt guilty, or perhaps embarrassed is a better word – in the dream I clearly hadn't wanted him back. It didn't seem the right thing to be feeling. I dreamed of him a few more times in the first months, sometimes comforting dreams of being held and loved, but also another one in which he wanted to return but I told him: 'There's no space here for you now. And I've given away all your stuff.'

Despite my sadness I did feel a sense of relief that I didn't have to look after him any more; it was as though I had put down a heavy burden I had been carrying for years. One of the many 'in memoriam' poems sent to me by his friends and admirers compared Michael to a kite snatched away by the wind. I pictured myself hanging on to the other end of that string, trying to keep him attached to earth, finally having to let go. Of course, when a kite string is pulled through your fingers it really burns. And now that I no longer had to anchor him I was suddenly floating free myself, unsure of what to hold on to.

In India death is regarded not as the opposite of life but as the opposite of birth – the end of a cycle. The death of someone close to you is, like having a child, one of the major rites of passage which change you for ever. You have no idea what it will be like until it happens. In the first days after giving birth, life as you thought you understood it is thrown up in the air, shattered into little pieces and scattered over the landscape. Everything familiar seems strange, like in the joke about the burglar who breaks into your house and replaces everything with an exact replica. After a death there is a similar feeling, as though you have to rebuild your relationship with the world molecule by molecule. One explanation of this I've heard is that the brain needs to reconstruct all the neural pathways, in order to comprehend the world without your loved one in it; this is a slow and painstaking process involving much repetition, and accounts for why grieving takes so long and doesn't progress smoothly but lurches backwards and forwards, so that it can make you feel like you're going mad.

Another echo of those first days of parenthood is the weird elasticity of time. You count it at first in days and weeks: a rhythmic pattern of ripples that drift slowly further apart – it's Thursday again, it's three weeks now, eight weeks. The days grind by as though you are wading through porridge, but suddenly whole months have passed. Many cultures have a pattern of mourning that reflects this state of mind: ritual visits to the grave are made at first weekly, then monthly, then annually; candles are lit, prayers said, grief revisited. In our death-denying society we are expected to put it all behind us and return to normal functioning within a very short time after the funeral. I was asked more than once whether I was 'feeling better now', as though I'd just had a bad dose of flu.

When something really terrible has happened in your life, you feel you ought to be immune for a while from further incident, even just on the balance of probabilities. But the reverse is true: when you are groggy, down on the ground, life has a habit of finding ways to kick you. Over the next couple of weeks I was pitched into new levels of anxiety and distress by a series of minor crises.

On the first evening that I ventured out on my own for a drink with friends, I came back at midnight to find someone had tried to break into my house, shattering the glass of my front door with a brick. Luckily a neighbour had heard the noise and interrupted the intruder, but I could not sleep at all that night, worrying that they might return. When the police finally turned up, which was not until eleven the following morning, they assured me that it was just an opportunistic attempt and I had good enough locks to prevent anyone getting in unless they were absolutely determined. But I felt as though my fragile defences had been rudely breached.

The same week I was pickpocketed in Oxford Street. In a way this didn't surprise me, though I had been trying to take extra care with things like money and keys, worried I might lock myself out with no one at home. You are more of a target when you are distressed and distracted – the same thing had happened to me when I was a new parent carrying my tiny baby in a sling. The stolen wallet luckily did not contain much cash, but the thieves used my identification to obtain a supermarket credit card and run up unpaid bills; this only came to light weeks later when I got a letter telling me my credit rating had been downgraded.

Soon afterwards my kitchen almost caught fire when an American friend mistook my electric kettle for an ordinary one, put it on the stove and set light to it. We eventually managed to douse the flames ourselves, but the house stank of burning plastic for days. The next day, a gutter at the back of the house collapsed and water started sloshing down the wall outside. I felt under attack from the elements – as if my overflowing feelings were wreaking a poltergeist's havoc.

One Sunday morning, Ruairi called up to me from the kitchen that there was a rat inside the guinea-pig's cage (we still had one of the original pair left). It had chewed its way in through the chicken wire on the door and eaten too much to be able to get out again. At first I panicked, but then I began to reason that, after all, a rat is just another small mammal. So instead of pest control I rang the RSPCA, whose phone lines are, astonishingly, open twenty-four hours a day ('If your enquiry is about a dog – press 1 . . .'). A kind operator advised me to put on gardening gloves and remove the guinea-pig from the cage, which I could then take outside to let the rat go.

The only flaw in this plan was the guinea-pig, a nervous creature who dashed from one end of the cage to the other to avoid being caught, until Ruairi just reached in and grabbed him. We carried the cage, with the little rat squealing and squirming, out into the nature reserve behind our house and opened the door; it strolled out calmly and began sniffing around. I couldn't help but be reminded of Michael and Ruairi's imaginary game 'Cat and Rat', and of my father's favourite character, the Water Rat from *Wind in the Willows*.

The effect of the rat incident was to make me feel much stronger. I had coped on my own with a situation that I knew many of my friends would have found terrifying. I felt ready to take on anything else life could throw at me, and as if in response the run of trouble ceased. The Steiner school Ruairi attended celebrates Michaelmas every autumn with a festival; the children act out the story of St Michael subduing the dragon with his iron sword, symbolising the strength we need to combat our own inner dragons and get through the darkness of winter. I felt I had been honing mine, with a little help from my own personal St Michael manifesting himself in ratty form.

I had coped with all the challenges, but my anxiety had been cranked up to a level where it seemed to have got stuck, ready to leap out at any provocation. Anxiety is a tricky foe – a very visceral response that is resistant to common sense and reassurance. Fear is an ancient and useful human response to a dangerous world, but it can get a bit out of hand. One morning on the bus I overheard a young man tell his friend that he was supposed to be at Gatwick airport in ten minutes. Since we were a good two hours' journey from the airport he was definitely not going to make it; my heart started pounding with adrenalin until I realised that *he* wasn't in the least concerned, while I was reacting to something that had nothing to do with me. I needed to get a grip.

Michael was a terribly anxious man. It was as if he only felt normal when he was worried; he used to joke that if there was nothing of more immediate concern, he could always fall back on the heat-death of the universe. I think many of our stress levels are set in childhood, at the age before memory, when we are totally dependent on our family and have to read and absorb their emotional energy in order to survive. Indeed there is increasing evidence that adult brain chemistry and the levels of stress hormones are strongly influenced by what we experience before the age of six.

It is extremely hard to unpick and recalibrate these reactions but, as often happens in a relationship, Michael and I had balanced each other, dividing up the tasks, both practical and psychological. He had expressed most of the fear and I had therefore become the one who was calm and reassuring, even though this was neither my true constitution nor my learned pattern from childhood. Now I was obliged to reclaim all the things I had allowed him to carry for me and learn how to deal with them in myself.

In practical terms life would have been far easier with supportive family nearby, but this had never really been the case for me. I always envied friends who could casually leave the children with their grandparents or aunt for an evening or weekend. My family had not played a very large part in Ruairi's life so far, other than the occasional visit (mostly of us to them) and financial support for his school fees. Ours is a small family and each of us was struggling in our own way, with little left over to support the others. My mother and sister lived fifty miles away on the other side of London, which usually meant a long slow journey. My sister, after working insanely long hours at her own business for many years, had become ill with Chronic Fatigue Syndrome: what energy she had to spare went on looking after my mother, who was now in her late seventies and in declining health. Michael's sister in America, with whom in any case his relationship had always been sporadic, had not been in contact since his death.

I did of course have offers of help from all and sundry – it's the first thing people say to you when you are bereaved: 'If there's anything I can do, you only have to ask.' And that is of course the hardest part. Who do you call if you simply feel too worn out to cook dinner? In our privatised society we all carry so much responsibility alone; I knew all my friends were overstretched simply coping with their own lives, relationships, work, children. Even when I did pluck up courage to ask, the response could be disappointing. In an initial flush of sympathy a neighbour had offered to mend anything around the house that needed doing, but when I asked if he could put up a curtain rail for me, he said he didn't have the time but would certainly tell me how to do it myself. I am reasonably practical, but at this stage I could hardly get myself together enough to change a light-bulb.

Sometimes people knew exactly what was needed. I asked a friend to recommend someone to fix my gutters, and she not only organised her builder to come and do it but also paid the bill. When you are struggling to cope it is these very practical acts of generosity that mean the most, lifting the burden off your shoulders for a moment. On the other hand, in my rush to accept any kind of help I sometimes found myself trusting in the wrong person, such as a decorator who came to price up the painting of my house, and ended up disappearing with the £100 I gave him to buy paint. I never saw him again. To some people the word 'widow' automatically means wealthy, not to mention easy pickings because confused and vulnerable.

Good friends did still occasionally come round to cook us a meal or bring a takeaway. One family in particular took us under their wing in a very special way: every Thursday while I went to college, they took Ruairi home from school with their daughter and in the evening cooked us dinner at their house. Later they would often drive us home, though we could easily have taken the bus. This continued every week until they moved to Devon a couple of years later, and it was the most magnificent gift – the closest thing to having family nearby. It wasn't just being fed that mattered, but having someone to eat with regularly. The best thing was that they enjoyed having us and said it made Thursdays seem special.

In the immediate aftermath of Michael's death I had found it hard to eat anything, as though I were completely engaged in the process of digesting what had happened. But I still had to feed Ruairi and, of course, keep myself going. Michael didn't do much of the cooking at home; his evening teaching schedule meant that he ate at odd times of day, or grazed from the fridge. But the thought that I was responsible for every single meal from now on was daunting. My mother used to complain that her life just seemed a long series of decisions about meals, and it is often the thinking about it that I find hardest. I had always tried to cook fresh food, give or take a fish finger or two, but now we frequently made do with ready meals or takeaways, and there was a low point when I sent Ruairi to the corner shop for a tin of macaroni cheese, which he then heated up for himself. I was so distracted that even when all I had to do was stick something in the oven I was quite likely to burn it.

Apart from the non-joy of cooking for one adult and one child, shopping for food when you are bereaved, particularly in supermarkets, seems to crystallise all your feelings of loss. Perhaps the extreme mundanity of the task brings into sharp relief how far from ordinary your life has become, and it's painful to watch all those families and couples living apparently untouched lives. Food is all about life – the dead don't need it. Things that I would never again need to buy leapt out at me from the shelves: products with punny names that had appealed to Michael ('Straight to Wok', 'Oat So Simple') or exotic ingredients ('Porcupine Sausages with Marmalade and Doorknobs', as he used to joke), and strange condiments, the mouldy remains of which I would end up throwing out. I took to going to the supermarket early in the morning after putting Ruairi on the bus to school, so that I could wander tearfully around the aisles without meeting anyone. The large empty store with its strip lights and the chill from the freezer cabinets seemed an appropriate setting for grief.

I had several house guests during the first months, and I found them very hard work. A newly bereaved person struggles even to get out of bed in the morning, let alone entertain. The stated aim of the visits was usually 'to look after me', but visitors require food and clean bedding and they want to sit up and talk half the night. One guest who arrived unannounced ('I hope you like surprises!') had me carry everything around for her, as she was recovering from an operation and could barely lift a kettle. Another complained that my towels were 'too scratchy'. Again I was reminded of the days after Ruairi was born when I seemed to be making endless cups of tea for visitors, none of whom even offered to wash up.

It was coming up to Christmas, which has long been the most difficult point of the year for me, though I know I'm not alone in this. I've tried to conquer it in many ways, including going abroad and ignoring it completely, but it still ambushes me with its glittery promise. Christmas for me is a time of unfulfilled longing, vividly conjured by the pile of beautifully wrapped presents waiting to be opened. They seem to offer the promise of transformation right up until the moment that they turn out to be just things, which, no matter how desirable, are incapable of making everything all right.

Nowadays I tend to let myself sink into the season's miserable embrace, trying as far as possible not to spoil it for everyone, especially Ruairi, who loves it unconditionally. Michael was also melancholy at this time of year, not seeing anything to celebrate in the inexorable passing of time. His childhood Christmases in the Bronx had often ended with someone getting shoved drunkenly into the Christmas tree. During our first few years together we usually had dreadful rows on New Year's Eve, more often than not in other people's bathrooms at parties. But I still worried about facing this first Christmas without him.

In this spirit I had accepted every possible seasonal invitation, many more than I usually received, as people were clearly taking pity on me. I suddenly realised that I would not have a single moment to myself for the month ahead. Worse, most of the events would involve talking to people I didn't know, for whom I would be an object of tragic but fleeting interest. I was stuck in a traffic jam in the outside lane of the M25, on my way to my sister's birthday dinner, when I had a panic attack. Sobbing and hyperventilating, I had to get Ruairi to ring my sister, who did her best to talk me down while the traffic edged its way round me. She offered to have Ruairi to stay for a few days so that I could rest; I managed to finish the journey, drop him at her house and return to London, where I spent forty-eight hours completely alone, crying, writing, sleeping and talking to no one – just listening to what was going on inside me.

Loneliness can be an important ally; it gets you back into your own feelings, which most of us spend a lot of time trying to evade. I walked in the rain in the growing dusk and thought about being alone – the kind of aloneness of the spirit that is part of the human condition. I think I have been lonely my whole life, starting in childhood when my mother's poor mental health made her unable to connect with us properly. She did her best, and from the outside my early life appeared to be a comfortable middle-class existence, but only as an adult have I become conscious of the gaping hole at the heart of it, which was that I never felt loved or wanted.

I also often felt lonely in my relationship with Michael. Partly, I think this was because no partner can fill the emptiness left by lack of mothering; it's what we unconsciously expect but it is too much to ask of one person. We long for a symbiotic union, but no matter how close you are to a partner you are still separate human beings, responsible for your own feelings. Once during an argument Michael said to me, 'You don't know me at all!', and I wondered: can one really ever know another human being?

I had chosen to love a man whose early childhood was perhaps even more unstable than my own, certainly more visibly so. Michael grew up with exile, poverty, unemployment, alcoholism, domestic violence, his parents' early deaths, all set against a backdrop of the dangerous South Bronx ghetto. Perhaps by comparison I could see myself as less damaged, or did I imagine that by trying to heal and nurture him I could somehow become the mother I had never had? But although two wounded people can empathise with each other, it can also feel at times like a drowning person clinging to a sinking rock.

Of course Michael had his own healing mechanism, which was poetry. If you live with and love an artist, you will always come second to their art. They can't help it; all artists are fundamentally self-centred in this way, and probably need to be if they are to give themselves fully to their vocation. They also often need a tremendous amount of love and support, both practical and emotional. Michael had a wide network of friendships and connections through his work, and it sometimes seemed to me that these friends, even people he had only just met, meant more to him than I did and that he just took me for granted.

But I realise now that much of this frantic sociability was an escape valve from his own intensity of feeling; he did have a few close friends, but if anyone really knew him deeply it was me. The curse of close relationships is that you often experience the worst aspects of your partner because that is where they feel safe to express themselves fully; the same is of course true of children with their parents. Nobody who only knew the cheerful, outgoing side of Michael could imagine the black gloom and inertia into which he would often sink at home.

My best friend from America arrived for a visit on Christmas Eve with her husband and son. After they had booked the trip, their marriage fell apart in a spectacular fashion, but for some reason they elected to holiday together as a family for the last time; her husband would move out of the family home on their return to America. I had also agreed to have my mother to stay, while my sister visited her in-laws in Scotland. I'm not sure I could have planned a worse Christmas if I'd tried. It's always good to see an old friend, especially one who you can really talk to, but emotions were running high and our children squabbled endlessly, although there was something undeniably distracting about being caught up in the drama of someone else's disintegrating marriage. We had agreed not to mention my friend's impending divorce to my mother, who in any case carried on in her usual self-centred way, as if Michael's death was a personal affront to her, a confirmation that her world was a terrible place.

My visitors were Jewish, but I somehow persuaded myself that they needed to experience the full Christmas roast, which I struggled to cook, just as I had struggled to put up and decorate the tree the previous week, in an effort to keep things 'normal'. On Christmas day itself we went to the Dickens Museum, which was the only tourist attraction open in London. As it was just around the corner from the hospital where Michael died, I decided to go and light a candle in the chapel there afterwards. My mother, exhausted by the outing, dozed off in a chair in the hospital lobby, so we left her asleep and went into the chapel, whereupon she woke up and had an enormous tantrum at being 'abandoned'. I don't know whether it crossed her mind how difficult this time was for me.

She of course had also been widowed, but instead of creating empathy between us it seemed to set up a sort of competitive grief, a battle to be Queen of Sorrow. She even told me how much worse it was for her because she had had forty years with my father, as opposed to my twenty-one with Michael. Also, she complained, at least I still had Ruairi to keep me company, whereas she was now completely alone. By the end of this conversation I had tears dripping down my face, but she either did not notice or chose not to see, moving on to something trivial. It was at this moment that I finally accepted that I would never get from her the support and understanding I desired; from now on, I would have to look for ways to mother myself.

That winter I spent a lot of time outside, tramping over Hampstead Heath or the bleak but beautiful Walthamstow Marshes. I felt that as long as I could keep outside in the light and air, I might avoid what was lurking at home in the dark, empty evenings. A winter landscape – silhouettes of trees and browning shrubs, damp misty air and weak sunshine – resonates perfectly with grief. I often sensed Michael with me on these walks, particularly in sudden flurries of wind – he always talked of 'the music of what the wind tells you' – but also in the intense stillness of nature. Once, sitting on a bench on the Heath in the winter sunlight, I asked him aloud 'Why don't I miss you?' and suddenly I felt as though he was sitting beside me, his arm comfortingly around my shoulders.

Watching Ruairi playing on Parliament Hill one day with a strong gusty wind, leaning against it and then letting it bowl him over in a somersault, I imagined that he was playing rough-and-tumble with his dad. On walks together we pointed out heart-shapes to each other – in puddles, in tree trunks, in the pattern of clouds – telling ourselves that it was Michael sending messages of love to sustain us. One time when I was putting laundry into the washing-machine, my eyes filled abruptly with tears, and the little lights on the machine all turned into glowing red hearts. These are the ways in which we conjure our dead.

For a while I felt an enormous connection with the natural world, in a way that I haven't before or since. I would look at a tree and almost feel myself inside it – the sap carrying me skyward to the tips of its rustling twigs. The cycles of nature – growth, flourishing, decay, death, rebirth – seemed more real and beautiful than anything humans had created or imagined. It was both a comfort and a distress to see this process going on as always, around me. Towards the human world I felt distance, incomprehension, even sometimes disdain.

At home I was drawn to sources of light and warmth: burning candles on the kitchen table on dark mornings, and in the evening building fires in the grate in Michael's study. One of my more spiritually inclined friends had told me after Michael's death that I seemed 'surrounded by light', and it did feel for a while as though I were somehow shining. But now I felt more like the poisoned Tinkerbell in Peter Pan, my light fading and flickering. When someone close to you dies you are for a while far closer to death than to life. Suddenly you are looking at life from the other side; it is as though you have passed 'through the looking-glass' and there is an invisible wall sealing you off from everything around. You can see the world but you can't really touch it, and sometimes it feels as though it would be easier to step over the line between living and dying than to find your way back into life.

There are of course many stories of couples who follow each other into death, unable to contemplate going on alone; it happened to my grandmother, who despite being in good health died only months after her husband. And of course some bereaved people become suicidal in their grief. A young widower I had got to know through a local support group hanged himself a year after his wife's death from cancer, leaving three children. It was immensely shocking and made me irrationally angry at first; it was almost as though he had managed to escape, leaving the rest of us to struggle on. For myself, I can't say that I ever actually wanted to die – I knew I had to keep going for Ruairi – but there were many days when I just wanted it all to stop.

That year the Boxing Day tsunami in South Asia killed thousands of people, including many British tourists. I shielded myself from the raw images and news reports of death and destruction, but although I empathised with the sadness of each individual bereaved family, mostly it seemed to me another example of the reality of death; that sometimes it takes us one by one, sometimes in large numbers. If you live you will surely die – it almost seemed to me that it didn't matter when or how. I remember, after my father died, wandering the rooms of the National Gallery looking at the old paintings, and all I could think of was that the artists were dead. It all seemed pointless.

The philosopher Kierkegaard said that life is lived forward but understood backwards. And it is true that, rather like in a mystery story that unfolds chapter by chapter, you only have the information that has so far been revealed to you. We can imagine how certain situations might feel or what we might do in them, but it is only in the experiencing that we discover what they are actually about. A close friend asked me after a few months whether I still thought about Michael a lot. I replied that I never *didn't* think about him, but that sometimes I thought about other things as well. He was not gone but still completely embedded in my daily consciousness, and I had regular conversations with him inside my head, his replies having more of the quality of feeling than of actual words.

It certainly seemed to me as though he was still around somewhere, living on in some way, though when I expressed this to another friend she replied that I just wanted it to be so, to comfort myself. Do I believe that something of us lives on after bodily death? I often feel that Michael is still very present – whether he exists as a spiritual entity somewhere, or whether he is so imprinted on me that he has become part of who I am, or whether his molecules and energy have been recycled into the fabric of the world, I don't really know and I'm not sure that it matters much.

People are always ready to tell you that what you think or feel about life is wrong or false, particularly when they have not been through a similar experience. But all we have in life is our own perception of it, which is ultimately our reality. We are like a group of people sitting around a beautiful vase of flowers: each of us has a particular view of the bouquet, which we take for the true version. Yet how can we assume that someone else sees even remotely the same thing, or have the arrogance to believe that our point of view is the only one? If I have a creed, it is that if I want my own beliefs to be respected, I must accord exactly the same level of respect to others.

This probably sounds foolishly relativistic, and of course there are plenty of people who seek to control or even damage others according to the tenets of their own faith. But faith changes through life and according to experience. Even strong believers are moved to desert their God when things go badly for them or they witness life's tragedies. I was raised an atheist; both my parents had found religious faith for a time but later lost it again – my mother as a young woman, my father during the war. In my teenage years I became involved with a Christian youth club, at one point getting both baptised and confirmed, but like my parents I also drifted away from the church eventually.

I have remained a spiritual seeker, but as with everything I seem to have to forge my own path. Michael, brought up with the incense and mystery of the Catholic rites, had a far more immediate access to the numinous than I, despite comprehensively rejecting the faith of his childhood. Reading his poetry now, it is clear to me that he expressed his sense of the mystery, of the eternal, through his writing. It was with some relief that I understood this; that, although always terrified of dying, he had made some kind of peace with it in this way.

Chapter 6

I had tentatively begun working as an Alexander Technique teacher, with a couple of pupils who had tracked me down through the college, as I had not so far done anything about advertising my services. One had rung me the week after Michael's funeral, which seemed a positive omen for the future, although I postponed starting lessons for a month, citing 'family reasons'. I was so nervous during her first lesson that I almost stopped breathing, but it seemed to go well enough and she booked some more. Having graduated from the three-year training in July, I still had to complete a postgraduate term at college, which meant going in every day to work with the students. Such a commitment was now out of the question, but they kindly allowed me to spread it out over almost a year and a half of weekly visits. It was a comforting rhythm that helped me feel I belonged somewhere, as I struggled to find my feet and start my own practice.

That August I had spent a week in Oxford at the International Congress of Alexander Teachers. It was the first time I had been away on my own for more than a night, leaving Michael and Ruairi to look after each other. I got a glimpse of life beyond motherhood; I was free to think and operate as an individual, to come and go as I pleased. Despite slipping on the stairs at home the week before and breaking a toe, I had one of the most enjoyable weeks of my life, staying in a friend's house and cycling around on a borrowed bike. The congress was wide-ranging and stimulating and felt like the perfect launch pad for my work as a teacher; Michael's death so soon afterwards rather took the wind out of my sails.

Valentine's Day in February coincided with Chinese New Year and we were invited to eat at a restaurant in the West End with a group of friends. Ruairi didn't eat much, saying he felt sick; when we got home he ran to the bathroom and threw up, then suddenly clutched his stomach and blanched, clearly in great pain. I rang NHS Direct for advice but the operator who took the call kept giggling, and when I asked her what was so funny about a child in agony, she told me she was being tickled by a colleague. Meanwhile Ruairi, stoic like his father, sat hunched over on the stairs, gasping 'I think I'll be OK as long as I don't move.' I put the phone down and rang the out-of-hours doctor, who said I should take Ruairi straight to A&E in case it was appendicitis.

It was by now after midnight and I tried phoning a couple of friends; one answered her mobile but was out of town; the other didn't pick up the phone, although I kept trying her number. It was clear I would have to deal with this alone, though I was by now trembling with fright. I simply couldn't bring myself to take Ruairi to the closest hospital, where we had had such a terrible experience with Michael, so I decided to drive to UCL in central London, which I hoped would not take long at that time of night.

Ruairi crouched in the back of the car, occasionally moaning 'Hurry Mummy!' in a frightened little voice, while I drove as fast as I could. I couldn't find the way in to the Accident & Emergency so I asked for help from a police car that pulled up alongside us at the traffic lights – when I explained what was happening they blue-lighted us to the front entrance. In complete contrast to our previous experience, this A&E waiting-room was empty and we were shown in straight away to see a paediatrician, who said he thought that Ruairi had twisted a piece of gut when vomiting, which can be excruciatingly painful. It sometimes requires an operation to untangle it but often resolves itself in time; in fact Ruairi was already clearly feeling somewhat better.

By three, we were home again and tucked up in my bed together. We fell asleep and I dreamed that Michael put his arms around me from behind; I said: 'Is it you?' and he replied: 'I'm here.' I told Ruairi about this dream the next morning, and he said that perhaps he had cuddled me in his sleep. This was the first time I had let him sleep with me since Michael's death, knowing that it risked becoming a habit impossible to break. He had never liked sleeping alone, and had spent many nights on a futon on our floor, or in bed with one of us while the other took his bed. This game of musical beds happens in a lot of families, and of course in many cultures everyone sleeps together as a matter of course. But I am a light sleeper and he is a wriggler; sharing a bed with him is like trying to sleep inside a washing-machine. I knew if I were to have a hope of being a decent parent I couldn't cope with such disturbed nights.

I have found as a parent that when I am certain about something deep down, it is usually accepted without a fight. Unfortunately I don't seem able to achieve this state of inner conviction very often. It's the grey areas, where I want to be strict but feel somehow confused or afraid of being unkind, or just a bit lazy, that leave room for endless, wearying negotiation and beating down. Although Ruairi still asked occasionally to sleep in my bed, he seemed to understand that my mind was made up, and in a strange way I think this made him feel more secure.

The body has an extraordinary way of surviving crises; it seems that the brain secretes chemicals which make you think that bizarre and frightening events are normal, an adaptive process that stops you being overwhelmed and allows you to cope. Maybe this was what was happening during the week of Michael's death; everything seemed perfectly all right in some profound sense, although it was clearly catastrophic. But there is a price – the effects of strain manifest themselves later, when the protective chemicals wear off. It took me a couple of days to realise how truly terrified I had been that night. If my husband could go to hospital and die there, why not my son? There is no immunity granted to the recently bereaved – I met a woman who lost her husband and two grown-up sons over the course of a few short years. Life is unbearably fragile, and for the longest time I was convinced that I was merely being prepared, as it were 'toughened up', for further loss and tragedy.

We lurched along, the days pervaded by a peculiar feeling of waiting for something, without knowing what. Waiting for the future to unfold? It was almost as if I was holding my breath until everything felt normal again. Or was it that my disorientated mind still expected to see Michael and was unable to make sense of the world without him in it? I read a psychoanalytic description of this as 'searching for the lost object', which I visualised as a constant rifling through the brain's storage network to try and work out what had happened, where he had gone.

Once or twice, after a particularly bad night or a tearful morning, I didn't get Ruairi in to school, but mostly we just kept going, day by day, although it felt like perpetual crisis management more than anything. I had a mental image of myself as a soldier between battles, leaning against a tree smoking a cigarette and waiting for the next order. The line between coping and not coping is perilously thin. But as the bereaved C. S. Lewis, in the film *Shadowlands*, retorts to a colleague who has told him that 'life must go on': 'I don't know that it *must*, but it certainly does.' Inexorably so.

People still commented regularly on how amazingly strong I was, sometimes adding that they would surely have fallen apart in such circumstances. Though meant encouragingly, it sounded as if they thought I wasn't grieving enough, or was holding it all in too much. But I had no choice but to be strong, to keep everything going for Ruairi, even though inside I felt shattered. Anyway, when I did let my feelings out publicly no-one seemed to know what to do with them; most people were probably relieved that I didn't seem too needy. I often found myself wondering if I was 'doing it right', having the feelings I should be having. Sometimes I was calm and upbeat when people expected me to be down; at other times a minor setback or careless comment would plunge me into melancholy or tears. Once, at an ice-skating party with Ruairi's schoolmates, I just sat on the wet floor and sobbed, while everyone looked on bemused.

There is a popular model of grief, based on Elizabeth Kubler Ross's work with terminally ill patients, which suggests that it can be divided into 'five stages' ranging from denial to acceptance. But I find this theory, or at least the way it is interpreted, too linear and reductive, implying as it does some kind of smooth progression. Grief is far too complex a state to be explained away by a sequence of more familiar emotions; it is more like an emotional landscape all its own. And there is no order to it – in one day, in one moment even, you can experience all the extremes from despair to elation. The five stages model can become a stick for others to beat you with – have you reached the anger stage, yet?

I read an interview with Nigella Lawson after her husband died of cancer. She told of her son, who was helping her unpack the shopping, saying almost in the same breath: 'I'm so sad daddy died'; then: 'Ooh, Twiglets!' She commented that an adult would not get away with such an abrupt switch of mood. But I had a similar moment walking through the local park and watching the spring unfold; the first spring which Michael would not see. Overcome with tears, I sighed out loud: 'Oh, Michael!' Then I spotted a tiny yellow narcissus – a lone specimen with delicate backward-flying petals that seems to survive and bloom every year right in the spot where it might get trampled underfoot. Suddenly within the sadness, I was full of joy at the beauty of life.

When you have just had a baby and your life is turned upside down, you can look out into the world and see others going through the same experience – particularly now, when the trials of parenthood are a popular subject for the media, and we're allowed to admit that it isn't all perfect. This 'mirror' helps you to make sense of what is happening and to feel that you are not struggling alone but are part of a shared experience, a bit like joining a new club. Being widowed young is a rare life event, one that most people will not experience, and there is no social reflector to look to for guidance through this uncharted territory. My life felt as 'unwitnessed' as the proverbial tree that falls in the forest: as though there was nobody to see or hear me any more, I was no one's concern.

Death is, of course, a major topic in literature – I find I can barely get two chapters into a book before a major character dies, even if there is no mention of it on the cover. To some degree it can be cathartic to read about others' grief, even fictional. But widows in the world of novels and films often seem to exist for one purpose only – to find love, usually within a year (or a few weeks in the worst cases), sometimes with their husband's best friend, whereupon it is assumed that they stop grieving and live happily ever after. If only it were that simple.

I joined an organisation for young widows and widowers, the WAY Foundation. My GP had suggested it to me, but I was initially reluctant to become a member of this particular club. On their internet discussion forum I read posts by people who had been widowed for several years and were still struggling, which frightened me. In the early days you rather hope that in a matter of months you will feel better, cope better, whereas in truth it is only the beginning of a long journey with many twists and turns. It is thanks to WAY that I have had companions on the road: some walking ahead to illuminate the path, some behind to whom I can give guidance and thus become aware that – slowly, slowly – I am recovering.

In our society there is a profound unwillingness to engage with death and grief, at least on a personal level. Germaine Greer, in *The Change*, describes how 'grief became first a private thing, veiled and silent, then a secret thing, and then a shameful thing'. Most people feel huge discomfort when faced with another's strong feelings and usually want either to avoid or to fix the situation, jumping in with suggestions or platitudes. ('Whatever doesn't kill you makes you strong!' was one I heard too many times.) Or they try to manage the feelings away: 'Don't cry, you'll upset yourself!' As if I wasn't already as upset as I could possibly be. Sometimes they simply run away; it is a common experience of bereavement that someone will cross the street or swerve down another aisle in the supermarket to avoid having to face you.

We have no idea how to simply bear witness to one another's pain, to just be alongside it with empathy. We have learned to deal in a similar awkward way with our own painful feelings. We feel angry with ourselves for 'wallowing in self-pity' when in fact we are coping with devastating loss and grief; the stiff upper lip is alive and well in our culture. Maybe this is why I've always loved watching the films of Spanish director Pedro Almódovar, where characters live in a technicolour soup of heightened emotions, tears running shamelessly down their faces. But I suppose this is taking it to the other extreme.

And I think there is something else at work, which is a kind of competitiveness. It's as if we believe deep down that if we are clever enough, make the right choices, make enough money, we can avoid pain in our own lives. Consumer society's emphasis on the 'pursuit of happiness', with its promise that if we buy the right product – food, home, holiday – we will be like those constantly smiling people in the ads, feeds this illusion. Another person's suffering strikes us on some level as a kind of failure, a contagion we would rather avoid, unless it concerns a distant figure such as Princess Diana, or a character in a soap opera. Given the popularity of gruesome crime and horror fiction, there seems to be a voracious need to see at a safe distance the worst that life can bring, along with a total inability to deal with it on our own doorstep, amongst our friends and neighbours.

To be honest, I have always found it hard to cry in front of other people – the best I can usually manage is to snuffle and squeeze out a few drops. I even find it hard to cry by myself; sobbing alone in my room I feel exposed and self-conscious, and also terrified that if I allow the tears to flow freely my grief might be bottomless. I sometimes walked around for days with a painful pressure behind my nose and eyes from the unshed tears, which also seemed to have pooled and solidified in my chest, giving me a tight bruised sensation as if I'd been stabbed. More than anything, I wanted to cry in the arms of the one person who was no longer there to comfort me; this is the paradox of grief.

A question I was often asked was: 'How is Ruairi taking it?' A child who loses a parent has to cope not only with their own bereavement, but with the grief of the remaining parent, which is another kind of loss. I had tried so far not to cry much in front of Ruairi, as he clearly found it so upsetting; I clung as far as possible to a brave, positive attitude. 'All shall be well,' we said together before he went to sleep at nights, 'and all shall be well, and all manner of things shall be well', Julian of Norwich's comforting mantra. Then one day I had a vision of Ruairi in the future as a young man accusing me of never crying for his father. After this I allowed myself to break down in front of him more often, reassuring him all the while that it was important to express your feelings, that I was all right, just sad. It's useless in any case to hide your feelings from children, as they live inside your head and know perfectly well what is going on. To deny it is just to confuse them.

Above all, I wanted to give him the opportunity to cry too, if he needed to. Children grieve as much as adults but they can manifest it very differently. We talk a lot about their resilience, their ability to live in the present and 'move on', but we are fooling ourselves; the wounds of a child who loses a parent are deep and lifelong. I might very well find another partner one day, but you can never replace a dad. Ruairi had not seemed particularly upset after the first few days; he bore the funeral almost breezily and went back to school, distracted and bewildered, but otherwise apparently able to cope. Once, he told me that a friend had cried all night when her dog died. 'My *dad* died and I didn't do that,' he said, obviously confused. I explained to him that some things are simply too enormous, too overwhelming for simple tears.

But he made sure to keep me firmly in his sight – if one parent could disappear suddenly with no warning, why not the other? At home he would often call out to me just to check I was still there, and when we were out together he completely fell to pieces if he momentarily lost sight of me. Even in the confusion of school pick-up time, I would suddenly see him being led sobbing to find me. Once, when we were visiting my mother's house, she and I had just walked out into the garden together when we heard Ruairi screaming out for us, in complete panic at our unexplained disappearance.

Anger is another way that children sometimes express grief. Ruairi had surprisingly never had tantrums as a toddler, but now he became at times a dragon-boy, an erupting volcano. A child bereavement counsellor suggested that he was asking for containment in a world that didn't seem able to hold him. Sometimes a good tearful rage can be cathartic in letting out pent-up feelings, rather like vomiting. (Ruairi has always been an efficient puker, on one occasion sending a 'waterfall' of mango cascading down the staircase.) One evening we clashed furiously over whether he could have another biscuit before supper. After raging and screaming for what seemed an age he finally sat in my lap and wept. 'I'm not crying about the biscuit any more,' he told me. Such a wise child.

Around the six months' anniversary I hit the buffers. I've learned that this is very common – the effort of holding yourself together becomes overwhelming and you feel exhausted and heartsick. I suspect it is partly the final wearing off of the initial protective hormones that are the body's reaction to shock. It is also the moment at which society seems to assume that you should be 'getting over it' and your friends feel less need to nurture and sustain you, and go back to their own busy lives. I spent the best part of three weeks mostly in bed, wondering whether I'd finally hit rock-bottom or whether this would only be the beginning of a series of 'downs'. When you have been hanging on, the feeling of suddenly not coping is rather terrifying.

Whatever it was, I had no choice but to go there and let it consume me. Holding myself up by willpower, 'keeping busy', as we are so often urged to do in the face of sorrow, has its limits and I had reached them. In the process of grieving – which is really the process of living – I have found that it is sometimes necessary to fall apart. To begin with, you think that if only you can put back together the shards of your old life – stick this piece back in there, glue it in somehow – you will feel whole again. But the pot is simply too broken, and a completely new pot will have to be fashioned to replace it.

This first 'crash' is the point at which many bereaved people turn to anti-depressants in order to keep going. But I didn't feel that I was depressed so much as depleted, wrung out – the work of grief going on under the surface uses up tremendous amounts of energy, unnoticed by anyone, including myself. Even later, when I fell into what I now see was quite serious depression, I held tight to the knowledge that I was grieving and that eventually I would somehow find a way through. It seemed to me that taking medication might short-circuit this process rather than speed it up, by blocking my way to the depths of feeling that I needed to experience if I was to heal.

What eventually pulled me up out of that first trough was an inspiration for the future, which almost overnight gave me something to look forward to. I went with friends to an open day at a beautiful Steiner school in Sussex, set in large grounds in the middle of Ashdown Forest, and suddenly I was convinced that this was where we should be, safely out of London in a rural idyll, where Ruairi could walk to school and breathe fresh air. I felt sure that Michael would have approved of this plan for his son's future, even though he would never have contemplated such a move when he was alive. There were some obvious downsides to my plan – we knew nobody at the school, and the 'peaceful' village actually had a busy main road cutting through it, but I grabbed hold of the idea and hung on.

It felt as though my mind had been constantly sweeping the future like an anxious lighthouse beam; now it had landed on this particular option, and since it was the only thing I could see lit up, it looked like the way forward. When Ruairi was born, friends had warned me not to make any major decisions in the first year after having a baby, and the same caveat ought to apply to bereavement. You think that you are perfectly sane and rational, but in fact you are quite bonkers for a time. Something kicks in – it may be the physical urge for survival, or simply our human desire to wrest back control from the unknown forces that beset us – and we are capable of misconceived plans and grandiose delusions.

The instant I had decided to move I could almost feel my roots beginning to tear themselves out of the Haringey ground, where they had been embedded for over twenty years. Suddenly I could hardly bear to live in such a crowded, dirty, noisy urban environment. I applied for Ruairi to attend the school and started scanning property sites on the internet, undeterred by the discovery that it was extremely hard to find a house anywhere near the school (or away from the main road) at a price I could afford. I was absolutely convinced I was going to move there and that it would all work out somehow. I began cutting ties, telling everyone we were leaving, and purging my house of what I considered unnecessary possessions.

I had a strange feeling of detachment from the past, which made it easy to dispose of material objects and even, it seemed, long-term friendships. Things were just things; they had no meaning to me any more, no matter how long they had been part of my life, or that they had belonged to Michael. One thing death makes brutally clear is that our possessions are not 'us', as we might on some level believe. As for friendships: three of the people closest to me and who had given the most support when Michael was dying, had told me soon afterwards that they were moving out of London, including Ruairi's best friend and her mother. At the time it felt like another bereavement. But life is all about change, I told myself; I'd had to let them go, and my friends, in turn, would have to do the same for me when I left. Sometimes I think that life is just a process of letting go: of people, of certainties, of the past. Everything is in a constant state of change and flux – even our bodies' cells are completely replaced within seven years – and all our attempts to fix things fly in the face of this reality.

I thought that we would benefit from a smaller, more contained canvas – friends and support networks around the corner, rather than a half-hour drive away in rush-hour traffic. I somehow forgot that I do indeed have several friends who live at walking distance from me, and that when you live in the country a lot more of your time is spent in the car. I also underestimated how long it might take me to find a new community elsewhere, having torn myself away from the one I have in London. Being part of a community isn't just about having your needs met, it's about being in a position to contribute; this would be enough of a struggle over the next few years, without starting completely afresh in a new place where I knew no one.

The fallout from Michael's life was still continuing. When someone dies, you suddenly gain access to the most private recesses of their existence in a way that even marriage does not permit. You are obliged to read private correspondence and root through personal belongings, which feels very much like prying. I was slightly afraid at first that I might uncover an unpleasant secret, perhaps a love affair. A friend of ours discovered after his father died that he had another family who lived in the same town – they turned up at the funeral. But I always thought that Michael was too disorganised to have an affair; for the most part I knew his schedule better than he did. Of course, he travelled widely for work and over the years several women had fallen for him, clearly seeing me as no obstacle to their affections – I dubbed them the 'panting poetesses', from their breathless enquiries on the phone. Michael was an extraordinarily good-looking man, and with the added magic that accrues to any performer he did not lack for opportunities to stray, but I think he knew how dangerous it would be to risk falling in love with someone else.

Long after you think you have sorted everything out and laid it to rest, things leap out to ambush you. Shortly before Michael's birthday I received a text message, arranged somehow in advance by him, reminding me that he would be fifty-one on 24 May. It made me jump out of my skin. Another day, when I was feeling particularly low and lonely, I came across a wonderful letter he had written to me, which I did not remember receiving although I found it in my desk. In it he said that if some supernatural judge were to ask him what was his greatest achievement in life, he would say that it was his relationship with me.

Later I would have some very old Amstrad computer disks opened while searching for Michael's early work for an anthology. (The company that undertook it billed themselves as 'Clinging to the trailing edge of technology'.) Amongst other things, the disks contained letters he'd written to friends, though probably never sent, during one of the more turbulent periods of our relationship. Michael was full of good intentions, even sticking stamps onto addressed envelopes, but he rarely actually posted a letter; hence his archived correspondence is rather thin on the ground. Reading these letters was like reading my own history from another perspective, or a private diary – slightly disturbing.

Of course, one of the main legacies of an artist is their work, and throughout the year I had been helping to prepare the manuscript of Michael's last book – the poems he had told me in the hospital that he wanted published, which were in a folder on the computer labelled 'Safest'. We decided to make this the title of the book, and the cover featured a photograph of Ruairi apparently floating in the night sky, a composite picture created on the computer by father and son. Although there were only twenty-four poems, half the usual contents of a slim volume, I wanted to stay true to Michael's wishes rather than pad it out with half-finished pieces or work that he hadn't considered up to scratch. He was always an absolute perfectionist, rejecting many pieces that would have been quite worthy of being brought to the public eye because he considered them weak or 'fake'.

It is quite a responsibility to be someone's continuing representative on earth. I had to make decisions about who could use his work and in what way, or even what they could write about him. There were things I wasn't given a choice over – a famous poetry prize was renamed in his honour, though nobody bothered to tell me at the time, until I saw it announced in the newspaper. I shied away from the biographical or personal, declining to be interviewed about our life together – let the work speak for itself, as he had always wished. And if they wanted expert opinion on the poetry, I didn't feel I was the one to give it.

I saw a cheap ferry offer to Ireland in the Sunday paper, and on the spur of the moment booked a four-week return ticket for the summer holidays. I wasn't at all sure that my ancient car could undertake such a long journey, but we had friends to stay with who lived in various beautiful places and we needed an escape. I planned to take some of Michael's ashes with us to scatter on a beach in Kerry, near where his mother had grown up. Besides, travelling more was part of my plan for the new independent me. I had always had trouble persuading Michael to go away anywhere, let alone for a month. He hated travelling, and holidays in particular; they always seemed to him a waste of time and money, and he was terrified someone would break into our house while we were away. On top of this, almost every form of transport made him sick. Our only successful trip in recent years had been our honeymoon in Italy, where, freed from the need to look after Ruairi, we were able to rediscover our relationship for a while and really enjoy each other's company.

Michael's family didn't go on holidays, as there was never any money to spare and his father was always tied to the job of superintending the buildings they lived in, so travel was not part of his emotional landscape, as it was mine. Their one big trip, when Michael was four, was home to Ireland in the hope of being able to settle back there; but the hoped-for job for his father with Aer Lingus never materialised, and after a year of living with relatives in Kerry and Belfast they returned defeated to New York. Michael's earliest memory was slipping and spraining his arm on the ship across the Atlantic. He retained extremely vivid impressions of this sojourn, particularly the smells of the Irish countryside, and his city-child interactions with the country cousins. He apparently once told some children to stop beating a donkey because 'It's the animal that brought Our Lord into Jerusalem.' And neighbours would be brought into the kitchen to listen agog to his tales of meeting the angels in his dreams – even at four he could spin a good yarn.

I had inherited the spirit of adventure from my parents, who had both travelled extensively, despite coming from relatively impecunious backgrounds. My father's army service took him to Europe and then to Egypt and Palestine, which he loved; he was a very good linguist, fluent in five languages, and never lost the bug for travel. My mother had, most unusually for the time, travelled around France by herself immediately after the war, and when my parents first married they spent a summer in Perugia together to study Italian. Subsequently my father travelled all over the world with his job in the civil service, sometimes taking my mother with him to swanky business conferences in far-flung places. When I was growing up we always had family holidays, initially in England, and later we took long driving tours through Europe which I remember in intense detail, despite having sat in the back seat with a book for most of the time.

After university I spent a few years largely on the move, returning home only to earn money for the next trip. I explored India, China and America, and was on my way to Australia when I ended up in Chicago, where I met Michael. When we first got together I worked very hard to convert him to the idea of holidays, taking him to Italy, Ireland and France. But he always became a totally different character away from home, losing his customary playful and curious self and becoming anxious and moody, and usually falling ill. I eventually gave up the struggle and started going away with friends or by myself, and later on with Ruairi, so family holidays were a rarity for us.

Once Michael's career took off he was obliged to travel much more in order to give readings and workshops. Even train trips within the UK were very stressful for him, but invitations abroad were a source of extreme anxiety. How I would have loved to go in his place! He did manage a creative writing week in Turkey, a couple of trips to Italian universities, and then, while I was pregnant, a book festival in Singapore. More recently he had been on a month's reading tour of Mexico, although he almost pulled out at the last minute, got heat-stroke while there and returned home quite sickly.

One year the BBC invited him to Nova Scotia, to do a radio programme about *Moby Dick*. Despite having an MA in English, Michael had read hardly any novels (he once confessed to having read 'bits' of *Middlemarch*), and certainly not this one. The recording would take place on a whaling boat, which he would find terrifying (he could not swim) and which would undoubtedly make him sea-sick. I had an image of a giant whale looming over us all summer like a barrage balloon, and put my foot down. Another time, when booked to go to a festival in Venezuela, he developed a suppurating eye infection which permitted him to cancel the trip at the last minute. How much simpler it would have been to say 'no' in the first place.

So our trip to Ireland that summer felt like a grand adventure, with luck the first of many, although it was also filled with echoes of the past. One of Ruairí's favourite parts of the holiday was when we arrived at Rosslare in the pitch dark after the ferry had been delayed, and I decided we should sleep in the car rather than hunt around for a B&B. He kept asking if we could do it again. I had brought a portion of Michael's ashes with us in a carved wooden box, but when we eventually reached the beach in Kerry where I had planned to scatter the ashes, it was high summer and packed with people. In the end we couldn't find anywhere that felt right to scatter him and in a way it was rather comforting having him in the boot of the car, not complaining and miserable as he would have been in life, but just along for the ride.

We drove through the spectacular mountain and coastal scenery of Cork, Kerry and Clare, staying with friends along the way. The weather was hot and sunny the whole time, distinctly un-Irish, apart from a couple of days of torrential rain. We spent the last few days on beautiful Inishmore in the Aran Islands, the westernmost part of Europe. One night I sang in a pub session there: 'A stór mo chroí', a lament for departed love. It was the first time since Michael had died that I had felt able to sing without crying.

Irish traditional music was such a big part of our lives together – the day I met him, Michael was playing the tin whistle and *bodhran* (Irish drum) in his band, and much of our early relationship involved me following him around to gigs. Having learned it briefly at school, I took up the fiddle, though I didn't have the dedication to play really well, while Michael taught himself to play the wooden flute, on which he had great style but not much in the way of technique. Our trips to Ireland in the past, usually to some music festival or other, had always involved long detours to seek out an ageing drum-maker in Tipperary or a famous whistle-player in West Clare: to touch the source, as it were.

The last time we had been there was with one-year-old Ruairi, to the Galway Poetry Festival, where Michael was giving a reading. It was there that we discovered we had left out a crucial 'i' from our spelling of Ruairi's name; it was the poet Seamus Heaney who put us right on that score, though there was a lively discussion around the table before they settled on a definitive spelling. When we returned home, we were able to have it officially changed on his birth certificate, although to this day it reads 'formerly known as.'

I drove seventeen hundred miles that summer, ending with an epic journey home from Galway to London in one day: Ruairi fell asleep in the back of the car and I just kept going. Arriving home from being away, or even from being out for the evening, is awful – the house lies in emptiness and the brutal reality of loss hits you all over again. There's always a part of you that expects to find your loved one at home and waiting. If you've had an enjoyably social time with friends, the contrast is even worse, and the loneliness more intense. Losing Michael had put such a hole in the centre of our life that at times it felt like we were living around the crater of Ground Zero, picking our way gingerly through the wreckage to see what we could salvage.

'Our Life Stories' . . .

Michael's career had really taken off, and in addition to working on a second collection of poems he had a busy schedule, teaching in London and travelling around the country to give readings. He was frequently away overnight and out at work several nights a week, often joining his students in the pub for a drink after class and rolling in long after I'd gone to bed. I was busy too, juggling my various part-time teaching commitments, which seemed to add up to a full-time job, though without anything like a full-time salary. Sometimes we seemed to be on completely different schedules that rarely intersected.

But life with a poet was rarely dull, and all sorts of things were drafted in to amuse us at home – we once spent the afternoon putting things under a patch of rainbow light that had appeared on the kitchen floor to see how they looked. Michael was a very funny man, always ready with a witty rejoinder or clever play on words; he took his sense of humour very seriously, if that doesn't sound like a contradiction in terms, and could probably have been a good stand-up. There was a long-standing joke between us whereby he would trick me into saying something that sounded vaguely like 'thanks' or 'thank-you' – 'tanks' or 'sinks' for example, whereupon he would crow 'You're welcome!' (He once took me all the way to the British Museum, just to have me read out the name of a Japanese deity: 'Tengu'.)

I was gradually taking on a managerial role in his freelance work: booking gigs, sending out invoices and doing his tax returns, which involved scrabbling around on the floor for tiny slips of paper and employing all my skills of guesswork. Michael found the practicalities of living complicated and frightening, and responded by ignoring them; he often threw away official-looking envelopes, including one containing a large grant cheque from an American foundation, which I rescued from the recycling bin. I was much better than he was at asking for money, or turning down work that was underpaid or otherwise unsuitable – I once hung a sign over his desk *that said 'No is a complete sentence' – but we both felt that it put me in an uncomfortable position of control, and at the very least meant I had to read his mail. He hired a part-time assistant to help him, but I had to do so much preparation for her that I soon concluded I might as well do it all myself.*

Turning thirty, like many women at that age I began to think about having children. I had known for years that it would be difficult for me to conceive, owing to hormonal problems, but imagined that when the time came I would be able to get the right treatment. Michael had assumed that, like him, I did not want children, so he viewed what he thought was a change of heart with trepidation. In truth, I'd always assumed I would one day have a family, but we had somehow never got round to discussing it. Many men are reluctant to become fathers, so he was not perhaps unusual, but his position on the matter was fairly extreme; he was convinced that a child would signal the end of his creative life – the 'pram in the hall' – and, on top of that, concerned that he might pass on mental-health problems to his offspring.

We wrangled over the issue, but as in most matters I eventually prevailed and decided to seek treatment. I was put on a series of daily hormone injections, and got pregnant almost immediately, but right from the off I had a mental image of the baby as a lone climber clinging to an icy peak in a howling gale, and was sad but unsurprised when it miscarried. I conceived again the following month, and this time the pregnancy felt strong and powerful – however, at eight weeks I began having agonising stomach pains, and an ultrasound scan could find no foetal heartbeat. The pregnancy was ectopic, lodged in the fallopian tube rather than the womb, and when the tube ruptured I was rushed to hospital for an emergency operation and a transfusion of six pints of blood. At one point in the ambulance I fainted with my eyes open and Michael thought I had died.

Michael assumed that was the end of it; that having risked my life, I would see that my dream was not achievable. But I was galvanised by the fact that at least my body knew how to conceive, even if it had not yet managed to sustain a baby. For almost three years I underwent a gruelling schedule of treatments, scans and monthly let-downs, which put a tremendous strain on both our lives.

Michael, a surprisingly kind and gentle nurse, gave me the necessary injections (in the backside) to stimulate ovulation, and dutifully managed to provide sperm at the required time. He wanted to help me get what I wanted because of his love for me, but his heart was truly not in it. Increasingly it felt as though we were heading down different paths which would never reunite. There is something appalling about looking into the eyes of someone you dearly love and seeing a stranger reflected back, though it must be a common experience in marriage. But I couldn't give up on my desire to be a mother.

There were no further pregnancies, and I was gradually becoming resistant to the medication, requiring ever-increasing doses to ovulate; eventually the doctors decided it wasn't worth continuing. Aged thirty-five now, I managed to squeak onto the waiting list for in-vitro fertilisation, although it would be two years before I reached the top. Throughout this time I kept hoping for a miracle, a spontaneous pregnancy, although as anyone who has had trouble conceiving knows, the relentless focus on getting pregnant is enough to kill passion stone-dead. I began seeing a psychotherapist, and Michael and I went for couple counselling at Relate to try and rescue our ailing relationship.

Meanwhile Michael's second book, Errata, was published to general approval, although not the kind of prize-winning acclaim that had greeted the first, despite being in many ways a stronger book: it's always hard to live up to the promise of initial success. He was now an acknowledged up-and-coming figure in the British poetry establishment, featuring as one of the so-called 'New Generation' poets in a controversial publicity drive by the Poetry Society that claimed poetry was 'the new rock and roll'. He accepted this accolade with mixed feelings, being now almost forty, the arbitrary cut-off date for inclusion in the list, and not liking to be pigeon-holed as a member of any group. He continued to travel widely giving readings, and had a growing reputation as a teacher – some of his students were now published and becoming well known in their own right. I carried on teaching music and playing in my band, but there was a baby-shaped hole in my life which I couldn't seem to fill.

With help again from my parents, we had moved into a three-bedroom house one street over from our flat. Now I definitely had room for a baby, although in the meantime I set up the room as an art studio and office, in case my fate was to remain childless. By the time I reached the top of the IVF waiting list I was already thirty-seven, and time was running out for my dwindling fertility. But I became pregnant with Ruairi at my first attempt, as though he had been waiting in the wings for the right moment. Against all the odds, I had somehow 'known' that it was going to work for me, but Michael, for whom the issue had retreated into the background, was profoundly shocked. Had he not been brought up with a Catholic sense of duty to family, and also still loved me profoundly, I think he might well have walked out on me at this point.

As it was, my pregnancy was one of the hardest times between us – I had got what I wanted, but at what cost? We could barely speak about it, let alone look forward to parenthood together. He reluctantly accompanied me to the ultrasound scan at sixteen weeks, but showed little interest in the baby's development, and didn't even want to feel it kicking. It was a bitterly lonely time for me, trying to feel excitement and make plans for the birth and the new baby, but feeling very isolated and depressed, with no support.

When we passed a crying baby in the street or supermarket, Michael would mutter: 'Someone's little bundle of joy!' 'It's just more life,' I told him. 'And you love life!' I was convinced that he would turn out to be an extremely loving father, but at times I wondered whether we would ever be reconciled as a couple. In time, he would thank me heartfully more than once for making him have a child, but for the moment things remained very difficult between us.

I had conceived, as it were, in hospital so I was determined to have the baby at home. It was a lucky choice, as Ruairi's birth, although ten days overdue, was so fast – effectively just over an hour – that the midwife only arrived for the last twenty minutes, and my sister missed it entirely. (Ruairi's pattern in life is to wait until he's good and ready and then just do it.) This meant that Michael simply had to step up; he spent a frantic hour rushing backwards and forwards between me, the phone and the hired birthing pool in the living-room, which stubbornly refused to fill fast enough. There is a photograph of us holding our tiny baby moments after the birth, in which Michael appears overcome with paternal emotion, hand on heart – in reality, he thought he was having a heart attack from the adrenalin of it all.

CHAPTER 7

We marked the first anniversary of Michael's death that autumn with a ceremony to bury his ashes in Highgate Cemetery. When he first arrived in London, Michael had trained as a tour guide in this old Victorian cemetery, an overgrown and mysterious place full of crumbling monumental tombs, which you can only visit on a guided tour. The training was part of a government scheme to reduce unemployment figures, but they didn't offer him a job at the end of it, possibly because of his inability to stick to the script, or sometimes even the truth. He at least got a poem out of the experience ('Privacy'), about the little bells that were rigged up outside some Victorian tombs, connected to the interior by a string, in case the occupant had been mistakenly buried alive. The last line of the poem reads: 'Sadly, these have snapped.'

I had imagined smuggling his ashes into the cemetery as in the movie *The Great Escape*, where prisoners of war in a German camp surreptitiously release bags of soil from the tunnel they are digging down their trouser legs into the exercise yard. But to my surprise it turned out to be still possible to purchase plots there, for the same price as in the stuffy municipal cemeteries where the graves are laid out in regimented rows. When I was shown the plot available, in an area they call 'The Meadow', I was delighted with its air of urban decay mingled with rampant nature – ivy, bluebells and nettles – which seemed to have something for both of us. Among those buried nearby were a few other artistic types and a surprising number of young people; I felt he would have company. And, who knows, perhaps one day he might even become part of the tour himself.

A grown man's ashes, the ground-up remains of bone fragments, weigh around six to seven pounds, about the same as Ruairi's birth weight. We had picked them up from the funeral director in a sort of plastic sweetie jar, but they had to be buried in some kind of urn, not just scattered or poured onto the ground. Having explored the limited range available for purchase, Ruairi and I decided to build our own out of papier mâché, moulding it to shape on a Turkish *dumbek* drum of Michael's and painting it in bright swirling colours with a gold 'skin'.

On the anniversary of the funeral, another beautiful autumn day, we gathered at the cemetery with a handful of friends. I read a verse from Tennyson's *In Memoriam*: 'Thy voice is on the rolling air/I hear thee where the waters run'; and at that moment a lively little breeze broke the stillness of the graveyard – perhaps Michael passing through? Then I played a slow air on the tin whistle called *The Scholar's Lament for his Books,* which Michael had taught me in Chicago long ago. Other friends read poems and spoke about their memories, and then the grave digger, who had worked in the cemetery since he was a little boy, when his father held the post, lowered the ashes into the hole and buried them. Afterwards we all went for lunch together at Marine Ices.

The first year after bereavement is a string of 'firsts' – holidays, birthdays and anniversaries – each a sharp reminder of loss and of the inexorable continuation of life. They loom in the weeks before like a series of tests that you have to pass; often the build-up of tension is worse than the day itself. I had experienced a varied cocktail of emotions: on Ruairi's ninth birthday (sorrow that Michael would miss him growing up); my own forty-seventh (the previous year, after being particularly hopeless at birthdays during our two decades together, Michael had surprised me by buying lovely presents and even wrapping them up and giving them to me on the day); and what would have been Michael's fifty-first (except that he was frozen in time, forever fifty). On Father's Day, which we had never previously made much of, Ruairi and I released a helium balloon printed with the words 'My dad's the best!' from the high terrace of Alexandra Palace, and watched till it vanished in the blue yonder.

On our wedding anniversary, which would only have been the second, I pinned a photograph of us on our wedding day to the 'marriage trees' in the nature reserve behind our house: a cherry and a birch which have grown to maturity completely intertwined. I felt like one of these trees deprived of its supporting partner, twisted out of shape and finding it hard to stand up alone. But on the anniversary of the day we had met in Chicago, which we had celebrated as 'our day' for all the years before we got married, I found I was mostly grateful and happy for the years we had loved each other. I tried, as I had tried all along, to stay true to what I was actually feeling rather than get swept up in the fear of what it might be like, or what others might expect me to feel.

The first anniversary of a death is huge, though. It feels at the same time a tremendous accomplishment to have survived a whole year and an astonishing reminder of how quickly time passes. And then of course the process doesn't just stop and things revert to normal – it grinds on into another year. Often the second year can be much harder; the anaesthetic has well and truly worn off and the pain is real and hard and ongoing. People pop their heads up briefly from their own busy lives to, as it were, salute your achievement in making it through a year, and then melt away leaving you to get on with it, assuming you are now 'moving on'.

As we headed into winter I could feel my mood growing darker and bleaker almost by the day. Suddenly I couldn't feel Michael close to me any more; it was as if I had buried his spirit along with the ashes. That familiar voice in my head which I'd been able to chat to with such ease and familiarity had vanished, and when I tried to make contact all I heard was an echoing emptiness. Grief had finally caught up with me and I missed Michael dreadfully. I began to be afraid that I might forget him, and to regret all the clothes and belongings that I had packed up and given away to charity a few months earlier. At the time I had been determined not to burden the eight-year-old Ruairi with all his father's possessions to cart around for a lifetime, but now I wished I had hung on to every earthly trace, every speck of dust that might once have been part of Michael.

It is generally assumed that as time goes on you get more used to the absence of a dead partner, that the wounds heal, but I think the reverse is true. Rather, as with an amputated limb, you accommodate yourself in time to the loss, but it never stops being a loss. A character in an Ann Tyler novel likens grief to giving up water. Unlike, say, cigarettes, where the craving diminishes over time, you just get thirstier and thirstier. How can it be better that it is now a whole year, or five, since you last saw the person you loved? This is not to say that you don't somehow get used to missing them and to the practicalities of living without them, though this also takes a very long time. But even when I think of Michael now the pang of loss is as sharp as it ever was, the sense of bewilderment as strong.

Michael's posthumous book of poems, *Safest*, was published in October, and there was a packed launch event for it at the South Bank Centre. Eight of his poet friends chose a favourite poem of his to read, and I also read – a poem called 'Our Life Stories', about snow globes, which contains the line 'Let's hold these sad toy storms in which we're held'. Again I felt no stage-fright; the memory of his voice and the way he had phrased it was so clear in my head. Several people came up to me afterwards and suggested I could make a career of touring Michael's work, but, although I had enjoyed the whole process of editing the book and performing the poems, I could think of nothing worse than trailing around on his posthumous coat-tails. Besides, nobody would ever do justice to his work as well as Michael: introducing the poems with charm and humour, and performing from memory, which gave them a sense of intimacy that was like having them spoken privately into your ear.

Since his death, I had learned that many people thought of themselves as Michael's special friend; he had a gift for reaching out and connecting to others which his son has inherited, a sort of golden charm that radiated from him. He was kind, attentive and always keen to put people at their ease. But he also wanted very much to be liked by everyone, and was tortured by the memory of people he had inadvertently upset or crossed. Sometimes I felt he did not set a clear enough boundary between himself and other people – they seemed to feel that he belonged to them. Or perhaps it is like this for everyone in the public eye; when the broadcaster John Peel died a few months after Michael, I knew it would be the same for his family, only in spades.

But underneath this warmth and gregariousness Michael was an intensely private man. His poetry, although undoubtedly springing from a very personal world-view, was not intended to be read as confessional or autobiographical, and it greatly annoyed him when people assumed he was the 'speaker' of the poems. This is not to say that there isn't a strong biographical element in the work, but it is well disguised. I'm not sure how much of his inner life he shared even with his closest male friends; like many men, their conversation seemed to consist mainly of competitive joking. He once overheard me speaking on the phone to somebody about a miscarriage I had had, and asked if it was someone I knew well – I replied that she was just a friend's secretary and he was astonished that I would discuss such personal details with a stranger.

Of all the people who felt they were close to Michael only a handful really saw the inner man, and like most partners I bore the brunt of his darker side. He could be extremely moody and was prone to bouts of bleak depression and torpor. It was hard to keep him going, both physically and emotionally; I sometimes had the mental image of myself pushing an elephant up the street. Although I made almost all the decisions of a practical nature for us both, the emotional tenor of our life together always centred very much around his state of mind, just as it had with my mother.

In the year after his death I was invited to many book launches and publishers' parties, which I found to be almost always dismal occasions. I realised eventually that I was only going to them in search of Michael, who was of course not there; and that I had only been invited because they really wanted him, and I wasn't him. People I'd had long conversations with at past events had no idea who I was without Michael in tow. When the penny dropped, they were sympathetic, but after a brief and stilted conversation I was usually left alone in a corner to drink my plastic cup of cheap wine. I stopped accepting the invitations.

That autumn I took up painting again, something I had done regularly over the years but stopped during my Alexander Technique training. Although I don't think of myself as an artist, in that I am not 'driven', painting is a form of expression that seems necessary to me and I miss it when it is not part of my life. I find the process of putting images on canvas utterly absorbing and often quite exhausting, but also very healing in the way it unites my thoughts, feelings and actions. But I don't do it purely as therapy – I also want to make good art. I joined a weekly 'open' class at Hampstead School of Art, where I could work on my own projects under the guidance of a teacher. I wanted to paint some of the dreams and memories connected with Michael's death and our life together, beginning with a picture of Michael and Ruairi from an old photograph. They are sitting in the glow of firelight, Ruairi on his dad's lap wrapped in a towel, having just got out of the bath.

Despite my strong sense that Michael's death had been somehow inevitable, I initiated a complaints procedure with the hospital about his treatment in A&E. It began with an exchange of letters in which the hospital guardedly admitted they could have done better in specific aspects of his treatment (the language used was that of 'failure to reach targets'), but their tone was very careful and defensive. Like many people who pursue complaints about medical treatment, I didn't wish to allocate blame or get compensation for his death; I just wanted to get a clear idea of what had happened, for someone to say they were sorry about it all, and for lessons to be learned so that no one else would have to go through the same thing.

Eventually I was invited to a meeting with the consultant who had been on call to the A&E by telephone that day; she remembered the case well because she had later had to debrief the young woman doctor who was so distressed. I told her that I could not understand why a fifty-year-old man paralysed down one side was not treated with more urgency and given an immediate brain scan. The consultant explained that the protocol in cases of suspected stroke is to do a CT scan within twenty-four hours, which in the case of a haemorrhage might well be too late. In addition, the nationwide shortage of radiographers, owing to the poor pay and status of the job, means most imaging units do not operate at weekends except with on-call staff, which explained the delay in doing a scan.

It became clear at this meeting how much more chaotic things had been behind the scenes even than what was apparent on the day. Once again Michael's notes could not be found, having been wrongly sent off in the ambulance with him and no copies taken. The email connection between hospitals had not worked properly, which meant Michael's scan results had to be sent over to the National Hospital by courier bike. It was at this point the National had refused to take him, saying that the haemorrhage was too serious, but despite this the A&E registrar had packed him off there anyway. He could have died in the ambulance somewhere on the London streets and I, on my way there with my friend, would have been none the wiser.

But could his life have been saved with swifter intervention? The consultant didn't think so – the damage was extensive, and had he survived the consequences might have been terrible. I was inclined to agree, but I felt his last day on earth might have been somehow less terrifying for us both if he had been better cared for. I don't know. There is part of me that bitterly wishes I had advocated more strongly for him, taken him more seriously. And then there is a part that says it was all meant to be: the failures, the incompetence, the confusion. It was his time to go and we were not supposed to save him.

In October, I took Ruairi down for an interview at the Steiner school in Sussex, which did not go well; instead of his usual bright and charming manner he was vague and distracted, as though he did not know why he was there. However, he was invited to spend a week at the school after half-term and try out the class. Friends in the village offered to put us up, and on the Monday morning we left home at the crack of dawn and I dropped him off at the school in time for lessons. He appeared to fit in to the class straight away and get on well with the other children, but after a couple of days the class teacher said he thought Ruairi was too young for the group and should try out the class below instead – in Ruairi's eyes a demotion. At this point things started to go seriously wrong; he clearly didn't belong in this younger group and began to complain loudly and misbehave. By the end of the week it was obvious they were not going to offer him a place.

In any case the countryside in November is a different creature. Every morning that week I had to dig the car out of a coat of frost to drive Ruairi to school. The mist didn't lift until mid-morning and, even though the forest was beautiful and serene, I wasn't sure I could imagine us living there. Evenings were silent and very dark – I pictured myself alone among strangers, lonelier than ever. The school, initially inviting and welcoming, had also turned cold; they 'did not feel they could meet Ruairi's needs'. We had been allowed to gaze into the brightly lit shop window but not to cross the threshold. I told myself that it was obviously not meant to happen, that life had something better in store, but it was a heartbreaking rejection all the same. On our last afternoon there I parked the car in a clearing on the edge of the forest and sobbed.

Whether or not we have a pre-ordained path, a 'divinity that shapes our ends' as Shakespeare put it, I can't say, but I have found it a more useful philosophy to try and accept what life brings than to live in regret and conflict. I was once told by a wise person that whatever happens to us 'belongs' to us, and I find this an empowering way of dealing with adversity: that we are not somehow the helpless victims of a cruel and meaning-lessly random life (which is my mother's attitude). Maybe we haven't chosen what happens, maybe it hasn't been mapped out for us – but we sure as hell have to face it, have to gather all our resources and take it on board. Of course, this doesn't mean that it isn't often harrowing, painful, hard, humiliating; that is part of the lesson, I think. It takes tremendous courage to live.

Even though at a deeper level I believed we had been steered away from a path that clearly wasn't right for us, it was as though a giant door had been slammed in my face. I was reminded of the years when I was trying to get pregnant; every month when my period came there was a dreadful sinking sensation of being back to square one, all that hope and expectation dashed in a moment. It was like waking abruptly from a dream to brutal, bare reality. Now the word that came to mind was 'aborted' – my attempt to start a brand new life for us had been thoroughly scuppered.

When Michael died I had felt free to choose my future again, no longer bound to the path we shared, but now I could see that the choice was not always going to be mine to make. It is necessary but hard to find a balance between having plans and desires for the future and allowing yourself to let come what may. If you take no action, then you are simply allowing life to sweep you along in its current; on the other hand, as the Buddhists say, 'you can't push the river'. I knew I had been trying to escape an unhappy present by immersing myself in a fantasy perfect future. And there is sometimes great value in exploring an option fully until it becomes clear that it is not the right one: it can help you to see what good is already there in your life.

However, that winter I fell into a black depression, filled with a sense of powerlessness and hopelessness. How far I seemed to have fallen from the days after Michael's death, when I was able to trust in the process of life, feeling that whatever happened was in some fundamental way all right. All shall be well, I was able to say, and believe it. Now I really came to understand the meaning of the word 'faith'. It's easy enough to have faith in life when you feel positive, but the real work is to hang on to that faith when you are at your darkest hour and there seems absolutely no light ahead. The only glimmer of hope was that this was again a necessary part of the journey of grieving, and that it would pass in time.

I felt shrouded in the darkness of winter, groping for a spark somewhere. I couldn't even force myself out of doors for a walk, which might have lifted my spirits, or at least given me some air and sunlight. When you are depressed the hardest things to do are the things that might improve the situation – they bring up such angry resistance, and you are so exhausted. Every morning I envied Michael: he didn't have to get up and find the energy to get through another day! I felt like there was a party going on in another room to which I was either not invited or, even if I might be welcome, could not find my way. I was shut out of life.

Once again I resisted taking anti-depressants; you need to take the tablets for at least six months to make a difference, and I thought that by then things might have shifted by themselves. In any case I have a stubborn desire to face what's coming to me unaided, which is sometimes a strength but has often made it hard for me to ask for, or even realise that I need, help. An employer of mine once dreamed that she and I were out walking together when I slipped and fell over a cliff. She looked down to see me clinging to a ledge by my fingernails, but I called up to her, 'Don't worry, I'm fine!' She obviously sensed something very fundamental about me.

In childhood I was never really able to relax into my mother's care, because of her unpredictable mental state – she suffered severe depressions and would frequently threaten suicide, locking herself in her room with sleeping pills or saying she was going to put her head in the gas oven, while my sister and I looked on terrified. No one at the time thought to recommend psychotherapy for her, and I don't know that she would have accepted it, though she was treated for years with numbing anti-depressants and electroshock therapy. She chose to regard her illness as entirely chemical – not her responsibility and nothing to do with unresolved feelings about her life.

In order to be close to her, I had to join her in her depressive state, and in so doing missed out on much of the lightness of being a child. I learned early on to trust only myself; I always felt grown-up and responsible and was outraged to be 'talked down to'. When I was expecting Ruairi, I asked my mother what she had wanted most to give us as children and her reply – 'a sense of security' – almost broke my heart. The sad truth is it was the one thing she could not give us. Brought up in London during the Blitz, at a time and, more importantly, in a family where 'negative' emotions were simply not allowed expression, she had most surely lacked it herself. How could she then pass it on to us?

A mentally ill parent is too locked in narcissistic torment to be able to support their child's growing sense of self in any useful way. Strangely, my mother was always at her best when we were physically ill – the practical simplicity of tending a sick child somehow brought her out of her own pain, whereas the expression of any 'difficult' emotions had the opposite effect. She clearly felt threatened or overwhelmed, and would immediately try to sweep away the feeling and then get angry if we failed to cheer up quickly. No wonder I grew up having no idea who I was or what I was feeling; it's something I struggle with to this day.

I survived that Christmas, which we spent at my sister's house, and crawled through the next two months, the pitch-dark mornings mirroring the blackness inside me. It may be that I suffer from Seasonal Affective Disorder, but something about having to get up before it is light during the winter months always seems very punishing. In February we flew to Scotland for a friend's wedding. As the plane descended through the darkness into Edinburgh I felt utterly and completely lost, as though I were floating out there in the night with no anchor. If the shock of Michael's death had been a kind of trial by fire, then this was like a trial by air: as though I were on a bare mountain top with the wind howling all around me – utterly bleak.

Weddings and family gatherings of all kinds are a special kind of torture for a widow, and unfortunately not the kind of invitation easily refused, though I had enough sense to stay away from funerals for the time being. At another friend's wedding the previous summer I had been just about holding myself together until someone said: 'The bride's going to throw the bouquet – go and stand over there with the single girls!' But I didn't feel single; I felt like a married person with a missing husband, an invisible shadow.

I've read that it takes about a third of the time you are together with someone to disentangle yourself when the relationship ends – for me that would mean about seven years. But I doubt that I will ever be truly disentangled from Michael. Our relationship lasted more or less my whole adult life, and formed who I am now; I think of it as growing up together. Even if I were to love someone else I will still always love him. And no one will ever know me in the same way: the person I was as well as the person I have become.

Many people liken divorce to a bereavement. But although the end of a marriage, especially if it involves betrayal or abandonment, is a huge trauma, there is a fundamental difference when a partner dies, because you still love them. It is like having half of yourself ripped away – you lose both the part of you that you invested in that other person and the part of them that you have taken into yourself. And although there is anger, it is more often directed at the 'cruel fate' that separates you rather than at the partner themselves for leaving.

But there is nonetheless a process of re-evaluation to be undertaken after a partner dies. In many ways you only truly learn how you feel about someone once they are gone. After my father died a lot of things about him, and particularly what he had meant to me, became much clearer – freed as it were from the static of his daily existence. Once someone's life is over they are 'fully paid up', their story is complete and you can see its whole trajectory and all that they contributed. It always amazes me to realise the huge impact each human being has on earth – the lives we touch, the endless ripples of contact that run out from us to one another. If only we could hold on to that sense of how significant and powerful we each are in our lives, it might make our time here seem more meaningful.

When you have been very close to someone, your relationship with them does not stop growing and changing with their death. It may sometimes seem that we idolise the dead and only remember their good aspects, but it is true that gradually the difficulties and dissatisfactions, the flaws and failings, seem to fade, and a person's best self shines through. My relationship with Michael had been complicated and in some ways difficult and disappointing, but it had also surrounded me with unconditional love, shared laughter, and someone who knew and understood me better than anyone ever would again. As a man who accepted and tolerated people with all their faults, he had not had expectations of how I should be, which in a sense left me free to be who I wanted. While determined that in the next relationship I would try to do things differently, I didn't in any way regret our years together.

Michael's publisher had said that he gave me joint credit for bringing Michael's poetry to birth. It's true that I often read the early drafts of poems, trying to look at the work from the point of view of the 'common reader' in terms of sense and clarity, rather than its more literary qualities, but I don't think this is what he was referring to. Michael was one of those creative people who needed a lot of sheltering in practical ways, and a great deal of emotional support, in order for his art to flourish: the archetypal absent-minded genius cared for by a loyal housekeeper/amanuensis. The whole business of living was a mystery and a struggle for him – money, accounts, time, commitments and deadlines. But his ability for organised thinking was manifested in his poetry, which is often formal and very tightly constructed; he always said that the limitations of form set you free. One critic said of his poems that they make you want to walk all around them and try and figure out how they were done.

I had always had my own work, my own interests, my own friendships. I thought of myself as an independent, self-sufficient, modern woman: compromising more on the domestic front than I would have hoped, but nonetheless in charge of my own life. It took me a while after Michael's death to acknowledge that I had actually lost the centre of my world. Without him, who on earth was I?

CHAPTER 8

At the beginning of Lent I vowed to try and give up being depressed. I wasn't at all sure that I could pull myself up just by an effort of will, but the promise of spring and the lightening days certainly helped a little. I contacted a psychotherapist I had been to ten years before, when trying to get pregnant, and arranged to start seeing her again. I knew I needed help, but had at first been reluctant to go back to the same person, feeling stupidly that it would be like admitting failure. Or maybe I was afraid that she would have forgotten me. My GP initially referred me to the Tavistock clinic but I didn't gel with the therapist I saw there, and realised that it would make sense to return to the person who had helped me so much in the past, and who already knew some of my story.

There is a section from Gibran's *The Prophet* that reads: 'Your pain is the breaking of the shell that encloses your understanding.' Losing Michael had opened up the chasm of all the losses in my life – my present grief echoing all my previous experiences of grieving, or of suppressing grief. I needed someone to guide me forward, because this was an opportunity to face up once again to what needed to be healed in me: the abandonment and neglect of my childhood. I had thought that my struggle to conceive in my thirties – five years of emotional turmoil and gruelling treatments – had been my 'cross to bear', but it turned out that was not all that life had in store for me. And, of course, that period had ended happily with the arrival of the longed-for baby.

I could only afford to see my therapist once a fortnight but at the time it seemed enough. I was working so hard on my own inner life that it felt as though I was being swept along a rapid river, surfacing every so often to check my progress and catch my breath awhile on the island of my therapist's armchair. My experience of psychotherapy is that when you are in crisis, it functions mostly as a kind of respite and support; the real developments happen when you are strong enough in yourself to start peeling away your defences and uncovering the next layer. It is not a quick process, and there are many times when it seems to be going nowhere, but I have learned to trust that, at the right moment, doors will open and take you a little further into both understanding and living with yourself.

Gradually I began to emerge from utter hopelessness and think again about the future. I asked a former student of Michael's, a young poet in his early twenties, to help me catalogue the library of books that lined three walls of his study. I hoped that they could be kept together somewhere as a resource for anyone wanting to study Michael's work in the future, but had no wish to turn my home into a shrine, as other writers' widows had done. Naively I expected the cataloguing process to be finished in a couple of months, but I had reckoned without both the young man's interest in reading his way through the books as he recorded them, and the sheer number to be counted.

Michael could not pass a bookstore without buying something – poetry, literary criticism, philosophy or any of his other wide-ranging and eclectic interests (*How to Talk Chimpanzee?*). Sometimes I would scan his shelves in desperation for something I might like to read, but there was precious little fiction, except for several thick compendia of sci-fi. There were more than a few unreturned library books from American universities on the shelves, although before moving to England Michael had visited at least one library at dead of night with a shopping cart full of books to post through the letterbox. My young helper's weekly visits provided a pleasant and supportive rhythm in my life: it was nice to have a poet back in the study, and he functioned as a kind of bridge between myself and Ruairi, being closer in age to him than to me. I couldn't pay him anything for the work, but he generously told me that he considered it an honour to help us in this way and seemed to be enjoying himself.

At last, after a long time of wondering where my connection to Michael had gone, I dreamed of him. He was definitely dead and 'haunting' us, though not in a scary way, and he told me that if we pressed up against each other I would feel his warmth. In the dream, I told my mother and Ruairi that he was only back for a short visit, but they seemed to think he'd be around for a while. I awoke feeling comforted – though I still missed him achingly, the sense of his continuing presence was reassuring.

At Easter we went away with friends to a 'family camp' in a big old manor house in Dorset, Monkton Wyld Court. Ruairi had a marvellous time playing in the rambling house and garden with the other children, but I spent a lot of the week in tears. Holidaying as a lone parent, you feel shut out from the world of families, although of course everyone was very kind and sympathetic to us when they heard our story. And it was good to be sharing our days and eating all our meals in company for a while. On the last evening we sat around a campfire singing songs, and later — when the children were tucked up in bed – telling dirty jokes, and I could feel my heart begin to fill again with the pleasure of simple companionship and laughter.

I had been looking for some way of helping Ruairi express his feelings about his dad's death, or at least have a chance to do so, since he seemed as buoyant as ever, although he was still having huge problems concentrating at school. He had occasional outbursts of furious anger, but it was impossible to tell what was just normal growing up and what might be a reaction to bereavement. Young children do not have the developmental skills to process things in the way an adult, or even an adolescent, might. They simply suck it all up into the growing sponge of their brain, in a very visceral and direct way.

I was astonished to find how little provision there is for bereaved children in this country; almost all of it is run by private charities or hospices, and dependent on where you live. In our multiracial London borough, which is a prime destination for refugees from conflict zones all over the world, there must be many hundreds of children who have lost a close family member, sometimes in very traumatic circumstances. They can be referred to mental health services for treatment if need be, but for many bereaved children this intense approach is not appropriate or even necessary. But this doesn't mean that they don't need support.

Eventually I came across a charity in Berkshire called 'Daisy's Dream' that ran weekends for bereaved families. As an out-of-county resident I had to pay several hundred pounds for us to attend, but I thought it was worth it just to put Ruairi in contact with other kids in the same situation as him. We parents spent the weekend with a group counsellor while the children engaged in creative and therapeutic play with a team of volunteers, many of whom had also lost a parent at a tender age.

I found the weekend intense and emotionally gruelling, especially since several of the families had lost someone to suicide, an extremely difficult form of bereavement. Sometimes the weight of shared sorrow in the room seemed overwhelming. But the children had a great time enjoying each other's company, with activities designed to gently draw out their feelings and memories. On the Sunday afternoon they had a candle-lighting ceremony, where even the little ones were encouraged to say something about their lost parent, and many shed tears – 'Even me, mum,' said Ruairi. I thought how wonderful it was for them to be able to cry like this, together in a safe and held space; it made me realise once more how emotionally isolated and repressed my childhood had been. Unfortunately, because of the distance involved we didn't manage to stay in touch with any of the families, nor could we benefit from the regular home visits and other support services offered by the charity. It was not until a similar organisation called 'Grief Encounter' started up in North London that we found more local support, but it came a little late in the day for us.

Later that year we went on a couple of weekends away organised by the WAY Foundation. Once again it was fun to share mealtimes and parenting with other families for a while, in contrast to our lonely evenings at home, but I found these trips utterly exhausting: long drives, sharing cramped accommodation with other families, and inevitably staying up late and drinking too much wine. And, of course, reliving unhappy memories and hearing others' sad stories. Ruairi asked me once why we all kept talking about dead people, and I told him that was what we had in common; it reminded me of the National Childbirth Trust tea-parties for new mothers, disparate people thrown together by being in the same situation. My hope was that being around other children for whom bereavement was a fact of life might make Ruairi feel more normal. But sometimes I felt as lonely in these groups as I did on my own.

In the summer half-term we spent a few days in our family caravan in Dorset – a creaky old structure hidden in the woods, with no running water or electricity. The setting was idyllic, but staying there was barely a notch up from camping, and as much hard work: fetching water, emptying the chemical toilet. We had been there many times over the years with Michael, who despite his aversion to holidays allowed himself to be persuaded to go on an annual family trip there. He enjoyed going for a run in the nearby pine forest, and bravely endured trips to the beach, sitting fully clothed as far from the water as possible. The summer before his death we had had one of our best holidays there. The weather was blissfully hot and sunny all week, instead of the usual rain drumming on the metal roof, and we built a small fire outside, sitting in its glow late into the evenings. Now it felt lonely to be there without him.

On the first morning we set off to drive to the beach and suddenly the car started to belch steam and smoke. It was obviously seriously unwell, and when the breakdown company arrived they said that the cylinder head gasket had blown and would be too expensive to repair. I function quite well in a crisis, and I remember feeling very calm, as if floating on the wave of events. We were towed to a local garage, where I saw that they had an old metallic green Mercedes for sale on the forecourt, in sparkling condition. It felt as though this car had somehow been put there for me to find (luckily I didn't notice till afterwards that the garage was called 'St Michael's'), and I agreed to buy it on the spot.

Michael had of course never been practically involved in anything to do with our cars. Being a native New Yorker, he was one of a tiny minority of Americans who didn't drive – being a poet, he was perhaps temperamentally unsuited to being in charge of a fast-moving vehicle. But I eventually got tired of always being the chauffeur and insisted that he learn; I mostly taught him myself, which created surprisingly little tension between us, although once he had passed his test at the first attempt he did not want one further word of instruction from me. Now, saying goodbye to the old car which he had driven felt like a further step in leaving him behind in our former life.

I was having difficulty now situating him in the flow of time; often I couldn't get clear in my mind what had happened while he was still alive and what came after his death. It seemed incredibly important to know whether he had been present at a certain event, or even seen me in a particular outfit. I remember something similar after Ruairi was born; I knew that I had had another life before his birth, but it was almost impossible to imagine a time when he didn't exist, and my mind would automatically slot him into every memory, like a composite photograph. Similarly, I now 'remembered' Michael in situations where he could not have been.

Memory had become a series of emotional bear-traps lying in wait for me. As he said in his poem 'Black Ice and Rain', 'the past falls open anywhere'. Almost everywhere I went in London reminded me of him one way or another. Places he had worked, restaurants where we had eaten together, things about which we had shared running jokes. A particular road junction always triggered the memory of a very ordinary argument we had had on our way to a party; it was like being haunted. In contrast, places that were not infused with his memory seemed to resound with his absence. I couldn't win either way.

I began to worry that I might forget him, and although part of me wanted him banished, so that I could go on with my new life unburdened by ghosts, another part wanted to hold tight to any tiny reminder, as if I were the keeper of the flame. I had a perpetual, very physical, feeling of homesickness, something I had suffered from greatly as a child every time I went away. But this time there was no going home.

It didn't help that I often felt as though I was carrying the burden of mourning completely alone. Although my friends had known Michael well, I knew they didn't miss him particularly, but were sorry for my sake. His own friends mourned him, of course, but we had only sporadic contact with them and the world of poetry, and almost none with his family – just the odd email from a cousin in America, and nothing from his sister. We had appointed a close friend of Michael's as Ruairi's unofficial 'godfather' when we got married; for the first year after Michael's death he had been wonderfully supportive, picking up Ruairi from school once a week and taking him out for lunch. But he had recently become a father himself, and we hardly saw him at all now.

I couldn't even share my grieving with Ruairi, who by now could hardly remember Michael, saying he was just like 'someone he used to know'. There were photos and memorabilia around the house, and one day we watched some old video footage of Ruairi in which you could hear Michael talking as he filmed, but mostly it felt to him as though there had always been just him and me. It's not really surprising that he had forgotten; children change so quickly that in a couple of years Ruairi had become a whole different person from his eight-year-old self. To be honest, I'm not sure how much anyone retains of early childhood, other than snatches and stray impressions; but I hoped that as he grew into a man he might start to remember a bit more.

All his life, Ruairi has said things that seem beyond his years, displaying a kind of deep perception; you might call him an 'old soul'. Shortly after Michael died I was tucking him into bed one night when he told me that when he was coming down to earth and choosing his parents, he picked me for my blue eyes and his dad for his sense of humour. He knew Michael wouldn't be able to stay on earth for long, but when he was born he forgot that. 'Our birth is but a sleep and a forgetting', as Wordsworth put it. But, of course, by now Ruairi had also forgotten ever having told me that story.

I was infuriated by a *Guardian* article about so-called 'married lone parents': women whose husbands worked such long hours (earning large salaries) that they felt as though they were bringing up their children by themselves. I wrote to the paper pointing out that you could not be classed a 'lone' parent if your children still had a father, even if your marriage was over and you were living apart. The irony was that I might well have sympathised with these women a year before; I had always felt that I managed everything for us all, and it often seemed an overwhelming burden. Now I felt that even an unsatisfactory arrangement with another parent, just knowing they were there, would beat doing it all alone.

Only a tiny proportion of 'single parent' families actually have just one parent. Most share the care of their children to some degree, and, while this is clearly a difficult and contentious area, at least the parents get time off and the child knows they still have two parents to turn to. There is also usually some financial input, even if only birthday presents or holidays. I felt that nobody understood the extent of my isolation. One friend told me that she found it very difficult when she was on her own with the children for 'her half of the week'. Another said that she knew how I felt because her husband frequently worked in the evenings. One of my widowed friends who has brought up her daughter alone since the age of four was told by a neighbour that he knew what she was going through because his wife was away for a fortnight – 'and I've got TWO children to look after!'

On top of all the practical complications of running a home, making a living and raising children single-handed, a widowed parent is also grieving and coping with her children's grief. This can feel like a double loss to the child, that the surviving parent is in too much pain to connect with them properly. Parenting is always relentless, but the hardest thing is the enormous emotional responsibility of this relationship in which you are everything to each other. Once, when we were away with friends in Norfolk, Ruairi had to have an emergency extraction of a rotten tooth and I knew that there was no one on earth to whom this mattered as much as it did to me. I felt like the last outpost in the desert – beyond me, nothing.

That summer Ruairi and I made another epic voyage, this time to the south of France in the Mercedes, initially staying with friends and then moving on to campsites in the Dordogne, where once again amid the holidaying families I was hit by my isolation. In between the constant work that is camping, I made the effort to chat to a few people, but it was hard to connect. I always felt I needed to explain my situation: not a run-of-the-mill divorced single parent, but a tragic widow. The trouble with this is it's a real conversation killer; either the recipient of the information does not respond at all, which makes you feel somehow invisible, or they become so curious and sympathetic you wish you had not mentioned it. I began to wonder – am I allowing my widowhood to define who I am?

One evening we ended up in a small-town campsite where there was a free wine-tasting for guests. I propped up the bar drinking *kir royales* and chatting to a friendly French couple, while Ruairi downed Coca-Colas and enquired every so often about dinner. By the time the sun had gone down and it had begun to drizzle, I was drunk in charge of a child, or rather he was now in charge of me; he solicitously helped me back to the tent, where I lay down in a daze, and helped himself to a dinner of jaffa cakes. I wasn't allowed to forget this evening of debauchery, though miraculously I awoke the next morning none the worse for wear. Clearly I had needed to 'break out'.

Strangely, when we got home, although we'd been gone over three weeks and driven two thousand miles, I didn't feel as though I'd been away at all: there was none of that feeling of refreshment and renewal that a holiday can bring, no sense of relief in the homecoming. I was still plodding along in the same trench, hearing the thud of my own lonely footsteps. I realised that I felt quite diminished without a husband – less interesting, less worth knowing – as though my value as a person had been tied up in the relationship rather than in myself, not just in other people's eyes but in my own. I just didn't know who *I* was any more.

It is very strange being suddenly single after twenty-one years of coupledom, particularly in middle age. The last time I had been single I was in my early twenties, and it takes time to realise that one has grown up: men of my own age looked positively ancient to me. I found myself looking searchingly at every man I encountered – from the washing-machine repair man to someone I sat next to on the bus – almost weighing them up as if they were applying for the job of partner. I even looked at friends' husbands differently, though not in a predatory way; more as you might look at someone's furnishings when you are thinking of redecorating your own home.

That autumn I had a first inkling of romantic interest – a divorced parent at school who I bumped into one day while out shopping. Rather as with my proposed move to Sussex the year before, I felt as if a light had shone into the darkness and picked out this man for me. However, it was clear from the start that he didn't feel the same, and also quite rightly perceived that I was still in turmoil and not yet ready for a new relationship. For a few weeks I was completely possessed by the fantasy of salvation in the form of this poor fellow; like a teenager I stalked him and engineered 'accidental' meetings, all to no avail. Abruptly, the bubble burst and I came to my senses with a huge feeling of relief. I went through the same thing again a few months later with another man – both times had the obsessed quality of being under a spell. Each time I found myself attracted to someone, it seemed to open up a void of loneliness and a longing to belong somewhere, as if just the crack of a possible connection exposed the emptiness of my life.

Some widows, and especially widowers, hook up with someone new quite quickly – I think of it as 'filling the empty chair' – but few of these new relationships last long-term. One problem is that if you have abruptly been robbed of a very intimate relationship you have overly high expectations of the next one, whereas new partnerships take time and effort to build. One widowed friend was accused of 'missing out a stage' in the relationship, trying to jump straight from dating to domesticity. I decided that the first task was to better understand who I needed to be myself; then perhaps I would meet someone who would be right for the new me.

'Our Life Stories' . . .

I returned to teaching for a few hours a week when Ruairi was about five months old. It is not always easy for men to take on the care of little babies, particularly breast-feeding ones, but Michael just about managed to cope with the demands of babysitting, though he always gave Ruairi straight back to me when I got home. Later we employed a lovely Argentinian woman to look after Ruairi a couple of afternoons while I was teaching, so that Michael could get on with his work – she became a very important figure in Ruairi's life, and we are still in touch.

My feminist ideal of sharing housework and child-care equally with my partner seemed to have receded even further, not helped by our widely diverging standards of housekeeping. Michael certainly believed in equality between the sexes, and did not expect me to cook for him or do his laundry, but he would have been content to live in a very minimal and chaotic way, which I could not tolerate, especially once there was a baby in the house.

But perhaps the truth of it is that I felt responsible for coercing him into fatherhood, and took on the major part of the commitment as a penance. In any case, there is nothing like the demands of parenthood to rapidly polarise domestic roles. Michael was by now the chief breadwinner, and like many women I felt that in this equation home and baby became my sphere by default. The first years of parenthood pose a great strain on most relationships, but after all we had been through neither of us could contemplate breaking up, and despite his reluctance to be a parent Michael was trying hard to adapt to the new life. One afternoon he put on the record of Sly and the Family Stone's 'It's a family affair' and danced round the living-room with Ruairi in his arms. I knew things were going to be all right.

I had always been certain he would make a superb father in his own way – when on form, he had the boundless enthusiasm and curiosity of a child. Once Ruairi had begun to talk, a strong bond of love and companionship grew between father and son. I couldn't always be sure that Ruairi was properly fed when left alone with his dad, but I knew they'd have a marvellous time playing, making up stories and creating imaginary worlds. I was good at the practical aspects of child-care, but I found playing incredibly tedious – I'm not sure I'd even been very good at it as a child, taking life a bit too seriously right from the start.

Michael had never been a prolific writer, producing a slim volume of work every few years. A third book of poems, Conjure, *was published when Ruairi was four, and returned Michael to the ranks of prize-winning authors, netting the Forward Poetry Prize and being short-listed for two other major awards, the Whitbread and the T. S. Eliot prizes. Being a father had clearly not interfered with his creative life. Indeed, this book contains some of his deepest and most mature poems, and also I think the most accessible: they read simply and with emotional directness.*

When Ruairi started kindergarten, I met a mother there who was training to be an Alexander Technique teacher. I'd had lessons in the Technique for many years, and in one of those light-bulb moments, I knew that this was what I wanted to do next. Michael agreed to my undertaking the three-year full-time training, as long as I promised to work as an Alexander teacher afterwards. He was rightly suspicious of my constant quest for new experience, which had taken me over the years into all sorts of fresh starts, including a stint in hospital radio. But, unlike him, I did not have a single driving ambition to propel me, though all the jobs I had done and the skills I had learned in my 'portfolio' career fed into each other: they were mostly about working with people. However, once I felt I had mastered something, I got bored and started looking for new challenges, which usually meant starting again at the bottom.

I began the Alexander Technique course full-time, which meant that Michael had to become far more involved in Ruairi's care, taking and collecting him to and from school most days. I continued teaching music as well, but, after two years of juggling all these different roles, I realised that I was not making a very good job of any of them, and decided to stop working during the final year of the course. For the first time I would be completely dependent on Michael financially. Fortunately, he was taken on to a Royal Literary Fund fellowship scheme which paid writers quite well to work in universities – it wasn't exactly creative writing, just helping students string coherent sentences together in their essays, but it paid the bills.

In the modern way, we had done things backwards – lived together, bought a house, had a baby, but never married. (My mother sometimes referred to Michael as her 'sin-in-law'.) Michael had always claimed that he could only go through a marriage ceremony under heavy sedation – in a weird presentiment, he joked of having a torch shone in his eyes to see if his pupils contracted, instead of saying 'I do'. Politically more inclined towards anarchism than anything else, he had strong opposition to what he called state interference in personal matters. A lifelong feminist myself, I held no particular torch for the institution of marriage, but the stubbornness of his opposition inevitably polarised me into the other camp at times.

Now that we had been together twenty years, I began to feel that a medal, or at least a certificate marking the achievement, was the least we deserved. Marriage was becoming fashionable again – several of our friends had recently got married late in their relationships, often for 'financial reasons', and it was, if nothing else, the excuse for a party. But at a deeper level, becoming parents had bound us irrevocably by blood. In the end it was he who suggested it, just before midnight on New Year's Eve as we walked back from a party together with Ruairi to the sound of distant fireworks: 'Shall we get married this year?' A casual proposal, but a major shift in our relationship, as far as I was concerned.

CHAPTER 9

The second anniversary of Michael's death was approaching. How could it possibly be two years already? I had been to the grave frequently during the year, sometimes taking a picnic lunch to eat up there, sitting on an old tombstone in the dappled sunlight; on 'special' days – his birthday, an anniversary – I lit a candle in a jar, or planted bulbs. It was a peaceful and strangely companionable spot, but still just a patch of earth, without any kind of memorial. A former student of Michael's generously offered to pay for a headstone, so I found a stonemason who could hand-carve the lettering on a simple rectangle of black slate – Michael's name and dates, the word 'Poet', and around the outside a line from 'The Present', the poem which I had recited at his bedside before he died: 'Make me this present then, your hand in mine, and we'll live out our lives in it.'

Michael's friends and admirers had continued to be generous with financial support of various kinds since his death. I had the sense that, along with the obvious sympathy for us, there was a feeling that he hadn't reaped the rewards in life that his talent deserved. Books of poems only sell in very small numbers, although he managed to scratch a living out of the spin-offs – teaching, giving readings, writing reviews – and won a number of major poetry prizes and bursaries over the course of his career. Usually, just as we were running out of money, one of these would come along to keep us afloat.

Apart from the readings, Michael didn't do much to promote his own career; he was ambitious to write excellent poems, rather than to be famous for writing them. You have to fight to get noticed in the arts, no matter how much talent you have, and in any case the rewards in poetry are few – Michael always claimed that 'Poet's Envy' was an occupational hazard, rather like tennis elbow. He was regularly invited to speak on the radio as a critic, and did occasional TV work, but his writing was perhaps too dense and literary for him ever to become a truly populist poet. Wherever he gave readings he gathered admirers, impressed as much by his personal charm and humour as by his obvious talent, but despite all the accolades his name was not widely known outside of the poetry world.

Had he lived, he would surely have been appointed Professor of Poetry in an academic department, like most of his contemporaries, but these posts have only sprung up in the last few years, with the boom in Creative Writing courses. Michael was by all accounts a fantastic and inspiring teacher of his craft, but he was suspicious of this new trend, fearing that it would become a self-perpetuating system, as in America, with its graduates going on to teach creative writing rather than becoming writers themselves.

His original ambition had been to become an English professor – what other job would pay you to read and think, he reasoned, apart from his holiday job as a night doorman in the Fifth Avenue apartment block where his father was superintendent. During one of his shifts on this job, a wealthy resident of the building had caught him reading Gerard Manley Hopkins, hiding the book inside his cap. She gave him a subscription to the poetry-reading series at the 92nd Street YMCA, where he would return to give a reading himself a few months before his death. He described this reading series as his awakening to the possibilities of poetry – 'my conversion'. But when he began studying literature at graduate school, he soon came to the conclusion that 'studying English because you like poetry is like studying vivisection because you like animals.'

A person's death day is as significant as their birthday to those left behind. My mood at this time of year is very unpredictable. It begins almost before I have realised it with the change of air from summer to autumn: suddenly I feel I am living in parallel realities, constantly switching back and forth between the present and the strange awful days of that week. The memories are also irrevocably entwined with Ruairi going back to school. Autumn always used to be my favourite time of year; it held a crisp sense of purpose and the excitement of looking forward to the new term after the formlessness of the summer holidays. But now it is tinged with melancholy and loss.

On the second anniversary I arranged for us to meet a friend and her daughter at the cemetery, and on the way there we bought a large heart-shaped red helium balloon to release over the grave. (Ruairi wanted to send up a firework, but I wasn't sure the cemetery authorities would approve.) By the time we got to the cemetery the balloon had mysteriously vanished from the boot of the car, as if Michael had spirited it away to trick us.

So began the third year of bereavement, which felt, as a fellow widow described it, like wading through mud. Throughout the autumn my health seemed to be deteriorating in strange ways. I caught one cold after another and developed a string of other strange symptoms: I had constant indigestion and woke up every morning with a feeling of nausea reminiscent of pregnancy, although it usually wore off once I got up. I also seemed to be losing strength, in particular in my arms and hands, finding it difficult to open jars or use a tin-opener. My scalp itched all the time and, although I wondered if Ruairi was bringing home head lice, I never found evidence of infestation. None of this seemed specific enough to warrant a trip to the doctor, so I just tried to ignore it.

At a friend's Bonfire Night party, an event which I always used to love, the fireworks made me jump out of my skin like a nervous dog, and it occurred to me that perhaps I was suffering from some kind of post-traumatic stress. It was as if the shock of Michael dying so suddenly, which it had taken me so long to realise or acknowledge, had somehow encoded itself in my body, resetting my nervous system so that I was permanently jumpy. Even the sound of papers coming through the letterbox made me start, and in the night the tiniest noise would jolt me awake, heart pounding.

Thinking that perhaps I needed a project to cheer me up, I decided to redecorate my bedroom and make it more into my own space. I painted the walls bright yellow, which made the room look as though it were full of sunshine, bought a new bed and reorganised the wardrobe space – now that I was by myself I didn't need so much storage. The room quickly became my private sanctuary, and although I had shared it with Michael for years I couldn't imagine how he and all his stuff had fitted in.

I couldn't face another family Christmas, so I booked flights to America to visit old friends who were going skiing in Vermont. A few days before the trip, I came down with a winter vomiting virus that completely laid me out. For two days I could barely move, and when we set off for the airport at five o'clock on Christmas morning, I still felt extremely weak and wrung out.

It was good to spend time with my friend and her family – they are Jewish, so it was delightfully un-Christmassy, apart from the snow and the masses of twinkly lights everywhere. Father Christmas had come to our house a day early, on Christmas Eve, so as not to disappoint Ruairi, who was still a fervent believer. We spent the last few days of the trip in New York, visiting the places we had been with Michael on our last visit, including the apartment building on Fifth Avenue where he had lived in a tiny basement flat behind the boiler with his father and sister. On our final day we pinned a photo of

Ruairi and his dad to the railings of the Central Park Reservoir, at the exact spot where it had been taken two years before. When would this memorialising come to an end?

A month after we flew home I was still feeling weak and again developed serious diarrhoea, which this time simply didn't get better. My GP sent off several stool samples, the results of which came back normal, but for seven weeks everything I ate passed straight through me as if in a gigantic purge. If I fasted the diarrhoea stopped, but the moment I tried to eat, it began again. Eventually I managed to bring it to a halt, but my body felt depleted after so long without proper nourishment and I had lost a lot of weight.

At Easter I flew to Lisbon for a brave little holiday by myself. I used to travel a lot when I was younger, often on my own, and wanted to try and reconnect with this strong adventurous self. But I discovered that a middle-aged woman staying in a hotel in a foreign city is pretty well invisible. I had the weird sensation of being trapped inside myself, like a driver in a vehicle – looking out through the windows of my eyes as I walked around and keeping up a ceaseless internal narration, like someone out of a stream-of-consciousness novel. Eventually I bought a notebook and began to write it all down, which helped to quieten the agitation somewhat.

Evenings as a lone traveller, particularly female, are by far the most difficult times; a woman eating alone in restaurants is unusual, let alone sitting in bars where you attract the wrong kind of attention. I can't take a book as company because the lighting is never good enough to read by, so I just eat and watch the other diners as though they are television. I missed Ruairi dreadfully – he was my 'home' now – and part of me wished that I had brought him with me, although it would have made for a very different kind of trip.

On my last day, sitting in a small restaurant in the sunshine with a simple meal of grilled sardines with salad and a beer, I finally came to a state of inner peace where I could stop talking to myself and just 'be'. I felt now that I would like to stay longer, simply experiencing and enjoying things around me. Maybe it was like one of those silent retreats where you learn to still the chattering mind: I've never had the urge to go on one, and, besides, living alone often feels like an enforced silent retreat.

It can be liberating to travel alone – free to take your time and follow where the mood takes you. On the other hand, it is nice to have someone with whom you can share memories of a holiday; I had no one to tell it all to except myself. Living alone, I often longed to share the details of my life, both trivial and important, with someone, but you can't really phone a friend to tell them how disappointed you are that the supermarket no longer stocks your favourite cheese, and it seems equally hard for me to ring and say that I'm feeling desperately lonely and sad. Without a partner you are brought face to face with yourself; you have to be your own witness.

Had I made this trip when Michael was alive I would have been equally alone, except that in my mind I would have felt attached to something, and therefore more secure. What is this need we humans have to belong – as though otherwise we might not really exist? Michael was so wrapped up in his own inner world that he rarely seemed to know or think about my life apart from him, as though unable to imagine me anywhere but in his orbit. If I phoned home from a trip, it would not occur to him to ask unprompted how I was getting on. I remember standing in a phone box in rural Ireland, a rainbow soaring above the rooftops of the little white village, while Michael at home in London complained to me about his haemorrhoids. He often had some kind of health crisis when I was away – one time he cracked a rib coughing – or did something crazy like overdose on very strong coffee, or, on one occasion, eating a jar of powdered vanilla by the spoonful, which gave him hallucinations. It was as if my absence somehow destabilised him and he had to do something in reaction.

Michael had a rather extreme side to his personality; I often felt that he experienced the full taste of life, in both good ways and bad, whereas I lived things more at arm's length, mitigated by an inner observer. One of his friends described him as living 'in beauty', rather like William Blake, whose every experience was imbued with great intensity and meaning. This may well be appropriate for a poet, but I think it sometimes led Michael to seek out stimuli in unhealthy ways, as if he needed to keep the intensity of the feeling going all the time, no matter the consequences. Of course this could make him tremendous fun to be with, particularly for his friends.

Shortly after I got back from Portugal I noticed that my hairline was receding on one side. Soon there was a significant round patch of baldness there, pink and clammy, and a couple of other bare spots at the back of my head. Losing your hair is quite terrifying, the stuff of nightmares – it brings up such an uncomfortable mixture of fear and shame. I was torn between trying to cover up the patches with artful comb-overs, and an obsessive desire to show everyone what was happening to me. If the wind blew the wrong way Ruairi would hiss: 'Mum, your bald patch is showing!' I developed a new level of sympathy for men who go bald, or cancer patients whose hair falls out during treatment: hair is an incredibly important part of one's personal identity, particularly as a woman, and losing it is a very visible sign that all is not well. Of course, everyone rushed to tell me that it was a symptom of stress, but I had thought I was managing better now, or perhaps I had got so used to a particular level of stress that I no longer noticed it. I thought it could also be a result of undernourishment from the two months of diarrhoea.

When people say that an illness is stress-related, it's hard not to read an element of blame into it: after all, most of us live with high stress levels these days, but not everyone's hair falls out. It is commonly said that stress is entirely in the mind – a matter of how you choose to react to the pressures of life and nothing to do with the events themselves. But perhaps the real problem is that we don't let ourselves feel the full enormity of life's challenges; we expect to sail relatively untouched through difficulty and tragedy, and everyone else expects it of us too.

I believe absolutely in the mind-body continuum: that our physical and mental states are so interlinked that our 'self' resides as completely in every cell of our bodies as in our brains. Every thought, every feeling, everything that happens to us has a physical trace that is written into our body's chemistry and neuro-muscular system. Medical science is increasingly uncovering the mechanisms of how life leaves its mark on us, but humans have always understood it – that fear makes you sick, that someone can die of a broken heart, that shock can turn your hair white. But when people use the term 'psychosomatic', they often mean either that symptoms are imagined or that the sufferer is somehow to blame for causing them.

It wasn't just my hair that I was losing; it was as though someone had pulled out a plug somewhere and my energy was draining away day by day. I slept terribly, as it were bumping along on the surface, and came awake every morning in a state of trembling shock, as though cast abruptly onto the shore after a shipwreck. My legs felt leaden and wobbly all the time, and I quickly began struggling to walk any distance at all, even to the local shops. Just getting through daily life began to be such a challenge that I found myself opting out of anything 'unnecessary', such as social events; life was once again reduced to the level of survival. Ruairi hated it – he was frustrated with my lack of energy, and of course terribly anxious at seeing me ill. In the way these things often happen, my Alexander Technique clients began to melt away, as though responding to my falling energy levels; I needed the work and the income, but I needed the rest even more.

The GP sent me to an endocrinologist, who said she didn't think it was anything hormonal so she couldn't help me. In our overspecialised medical system, diagnosis is a long and tortuous business: you set off along a track to a particular clinician who tells you 'Sorry, not my problem!', whereupon you have to retrace your steps and start out again on a different path. Siri Hustvedt in *The Shaking Woman* calls this 'disciplinary windows that narrow the view'. My doctor seemed to regard me more as a collection of parts than as a whole – alopecia, indigestion, fatigue – treating each as a separate condition. But to me it was clear that my body was having its own kind of total breakdown.

Having at first inherited, or perhaps reclaimed, what I saw as Michael's anxiety, I now seemed to have taken on his hypochondria; or rather, since I was truly ill, an obsessive concern with the minutiae of my symptoms. I became focused on the moment-to-moment subtle changes in my body, noticing every little detail, every new symptom, however minor, and trying to build up a cohesive picture of what was happening to me. I spent fruitless hours on the internet – the 'drunken librarian', as someone called it – learning that my symptoms could be part of any number of serious illnesses, but did not really indicate any particular one. The strange specific symptoms didn't seem to be listed, or else I never found the right search words for them: the weird buzzing in my legs when I lay down at night, as though I was plugged into an electric current; the constant tight knot in my stomach, as if I had swallowed a stone.

My sister, who had had Chronic Fatigue Syndrome for years, was more helpful. Although I resisted the idea of having a 'syndrome' and felt that the pattern of my illness was rather different from hers, she taught me a lot about how to deal with extreme fatigue. If you have never looked at a flight of stairs and seen a mountain to be climbed, you will not understand what it is like to have so little energy that even making a cup of tea is a major challenge, let alone running a household and mothering a child. We have almost lost the understanding of illness and rest – think of all those wasted Victorian ladies who spent their lives on a couch. Now we are expected to take a few vitamins and battle on through, or to exercise our way out of illness. 'Why don't you go swimming a couple of times a week?' a friend suggested, when I told her I was finding it hard to stand for any length of time. I could no more have gone swimming than run a marathon – even the effort needed to get myself to the pool and undress would have been too much.

For years I had ignored my body's signals and kept going when I really needed to stop, but now I was being forced to listen. With this kind of illness it is essential to pace yourself; if I knew something demanding was coming up, I tried to harvest energy in advance by resting. Unlike ordinary tiredness, where you are able to recuperate quickly, you often feel no better when resting. And there is a temptation when you do get a little energy to run with it, because a burst of activity creates a surge of adrenalin that feels momentarily like wellness. But you are using up depleted reserves and will pay for it afterwards.

I spent much of each day lying down while Ruairi was at school, my bed becoming a sort of nest from which I conducted life at one remove. During this time, I assessed my life in terms of what gave me energy and what cost energy – 'sources' and 'drains'. There is always a balance between the two, but when you are ill you can't afford many 'drains'. I was still giving piano lessons to a couple of children – both charming girls and quite musical – but I found it the hardest hour of the week; I simply wasn't committed to teaching them any more, and decided to stop. Almost immediately, I began to play the piano again for my own enjoyment, which I hadn't done for years, as if my love of music had been dammed up behind the obligation to teach it and I had suddenly pulled out the stopper.

I tentatively started composing songs, and for a few months they seemed to come pouring out of me. While Michael was alive I could not have allowed myself to write lyrics – he was the wordsmith, after all – but now I discovered that the melding of words and music was a powerful means of expression, more direct than painting and very cathartic. Some of my songs were so sad that I sobbed my way through them every time. I also set a couple of Michael's poems to music: a tricky challenge since poems – his in particular – have their own internal music and rhythm, which needs to be preserved, otherwise you are just stealing the poet's words for your own purpose. I hope he would have been pleased with my efforts.

I was by now really ill and hardly able to cope. I felt more isolated than ever; there was a persistent fantasy at the back of my mind that there must be *someone* who I could turn to, someone who could look after me, but the truth is there was nobody. My sister was ill herself and trying to support my mother, who was by now showing signs of dementia; she lived alone and needed daily visits. Friends helped me out if they were able, but again I fell foul of the problem that I find it hard to ask for what I need, and also that asking itself takes energy.

My GP seemed to have given up on me, or was perhaps frustrated that she simply didn't know what to do – 'We all get tired sometimes,' she sighed. But I knew I needed serious help, and most of all a break from responsibility. In the summer holidays I sent Ruairi off to a residential camp on his own for the first time, and a generous friend paid for me to spend two weeks at Park Attwood, a clinic for anthroposophical medicine, set in glorious sweeping grounds in Worcestershire. It had the sleepy atmosphere of a convalescent home; the staff were tremendously kind and caring, and had plenty of time to spend getting to know you and helping you to get well. After my initial interview with the doctor, which lasted two hours, I cried with relief – finally someone was actually treating me as a person with a history, not just a list of physical symptoms.

Anthroposophical medicine, based on the philosophy of Rudolf Steiner, treats illness as part of your life's journey, a challenge to be faced rather than to be wished away. You are supported through this process with a variety of treatments: massage, hydrotherapy, herbal and homeopathic medicines, art and movement therapy, counselling, delicious wholesome food, and, above all, rest. The days at the clinic had a gentle rhythm that included a simple 'grace' at every meal and an obligatory nap after lunch. In the evening the nurses massaged your feet in order to help you relax into sleep. No longer having the burden of looking after myself and Ruairi, not having to think about meals or even laundry, allowed me to sink more completely into being ill; I mostly stayed in bed, feeling the need to be very quiet and introspective.

The doctor at Park Attwood said she thought that I was not quite fully 'living in myself'. I do often feel that I dissociate from reality, and as a child I would frequently drift off into day-dreaming until my mother would call me back to earth. Michael's dying had given me for a short while a sense of being fully real, completely in the 'here and now', as if an out-of-focus picture had suddenly become sharp and clear. I also felt like this when giving birth to Ruairi; it was a dramatically earthy and real experience, totally unlike the transcendental moment I was expecting. But the shock of Michael's death seemed also to have fractured something inside me, just as it had split apart my life.

One day I lay in bed sobbing, and found a place inside me that did not want to go on living: a dark, hard, bleak place that was at once deeply familiar and deeply hidden, like a black hole at my centre. It was different from the grief I felt for Michael, and I knew that it had always been there; I was grieving for myself, for my unwelcoming and often terrifying childhood, for the lonely struggle that my life had often seemed. It took all my emotional courage to simply stay with that feeling, curled up on the bed like a child, until it subsided. This painful day was an important turning point, and by the time I left the clinic a week later, thrust abruptly back into the challenge and noise of the real world, I had faith that somehow I would be able to find my way back to health, even if it took a long time.

In a world where many people live terribly hard and brutal lives, it is difficult to allow yourself to feel your own pain. I grew up in an outwardly functional family where everything that was wrong happened under the surface, unspoken and unacknowledged. I'm sure this is partly why I was drawn to Michael, whose childhood held far more tangible difficulties; it was a way of externalising my own inner pain, a kind of emotional pornography. When I think of his harsh beginnings, I find it extraordinary what he managed to make of his life, thanks to his intelligence and creativity, and his beautiful spirit. (Though I know he would have countered that he may have grown up in the ghetto, but it was the ghetto of one of the most prosperous cities on the planet.)

But I've come to understand that if we deny our own pain we in some way deny the existence of pain in the world. Perhaps it seems selfish to dwell on your own troubles in the face of the overwhelming hardship of others, but if we don't honour our own feelings we are in some fundamental way dishonouring or distorting the sum of human experience. As Oscar Wilde put it in *De Profundis*, 'Where there is sorrow, there is holy ground.' Sorrow and joy are essential to each other's existence, like the ocean and the land, or the balance in the yin and yang symbol, where inside the light there is a spot of darkness and inside the darkness, light.

CHAPTER 10

The start of the school year saw the third anniversary of Michael's death; I had not made any plans for it this year and everyone else seemed to have forgotten. Ruairi was not keen on visiting Michael's grave, finding it 'spooky', so I decided to do something more celebratory to mark the day, taking him to London Zoo, where he and Michael had often gone to visit the chimpanzees. However, the zoo now seemed to contain more people and gift shops than animals – the chimps were no longer there – and walking around in the heat was exhausting. I came away feeling once again that I could not be the energetic enthusiastic parent Ruairi needed.

I had never felt more alone. My illness seemed to have plunged me into a kind of echoing silence – the phone almost never rang, and it seemed we were no longer included in other people's plans, after the many times I had had to cancel. I felt quite angry with my friends. When I was first widowed everyone had rallied round, but now they didn't seem to understand or care. I was still a single parent, still coping with grief, and now dealing with debilitating exhaustion. Perhaps they just had 'compassion fatigue'? Or maybe it's that the daily impact of chronic illness is difficult to communicate and to comprehend. After all, when people saw me it was usually because I was feeling well enough to be out, so I probably looked all right to them. And long-term illness doesn't have the drama associated with death.

I longed for someone to scoop me up and take care of me. But why should they? There is a saying that 'to have a friend, you must be a friend', but I was struggling so hard to cope with my own life that I had little energy to spare for others. It's clear also that strength attracts and weakness repels in relationships; my neediness may have been driving people away. Parents of Ruairi's schoolfriends helped out, but I saw that they had organised themselves into mutually supportive networks ages ago, and I was somehow out on my own, a wild card. Not since my teens have I been part of a group of friends who all know each other – I tend to have individual friends who are not connected, more like the spokes of a wheel than the strands of a web. I think perhaps this puts more strain on each bond, as it is not supported by a broader network.

Friendships are fragile; they can seem so strong and permanent for a while, but then evaporate with a move away, a change of life circumstances, or a falling out. When my best friend from school got married and emigrated to New Zealand, I understood with sadness that the relationship with a partner would always come before that with a friend. It's no wonder that we depend so heavily on partners and the nuclear family – they seem to offer some promise of continuity in our lives, and for those on the outside there is a sense of not quite belonging anywhere.

Bereavement often leads to the end of friendships, even close ones; sometimes there is a big bust-up, but more often it's a process of gradual attrition. A major loss changes you profoundly as a person, and not everyone is willing or able to stick around. Michael and I mostly had our own friends and didn't socialise as a couple, so I didn't expect that his friends would want to stay close to me, but I was surprised to find that some of my own – people who had been in my life a very long time – simply dropped away, despite my best efforts to keep in contact. It was almost as though I had died along with Michael.

Perhaps this is just what happens in the course of life: people move on, lose touch. But in my vulnerability every friendship gone was an anchor cut loose, a link with my past broken. Fortunately life crises often bring new opportunities for friendship – I had made a couple of new close friends through the WAY Foundation, who understood from experience what I was going through without my having to explain it to them. The bleak experience of that third anniversary galvanised me somewhat – if I was going to be alone, so be it. I would be like a wilderness explorer or a mountain climber, reliant only on myself. I would stop agonising about being abandoned, and draw together all my inner strength and courage to keep going. Illness and grief are solitary paths, and it was no use expecting other people to walk them with me.

In a society that virtually denies the existence of death, most people would rather not think about it for long, and perhaps this is why they detach themselves from the bereaved, trying to put a safe distance between themselves and a sense of their own mortality, or that of their loved ones. We are shielded from direct experience of death; it is something that happens in hospitals, on television news, to other people. Because of this, the first death we have to deal with personally is likely to be someone very important to us – my father's death when I was forty was the first time as an adult that I came face to face with the mystery of someone you love disappearing. Losing a parent, although in some ways it is something you prepare for all your life, is rather like losing a leg, or half of who you are. My father was seventy-five and had been in declining health for years; his kidneys were barely functioning and the post-mortem showed that myriad small strokes had left him with curious holes in the brain function, a condition known as multi-infarct dementia. Yet somehow we none of us, including he himself, expected him to die just yet. No matter how much you think you are prepared for someone's death, it still always comes as a profound puzzle; in our very beings we simply cannot comprehend ceasing to exist. Simone de Beauvoir, writing of her elderly mother's death from cancer in *A Very Easy Death*, says: 'Foreseeing is not knowing. The shock was as violent as if we had not known it at all.'

One morning after my father died I was sitting on the stairs crying, and Ruairi, who was not yet three, asked why I was upset. I told him that I missed my daddy and he patted my arm saying, 'Don't worry, he'll come back', as one would reassure a small child. Young children have no concept of the finality of death, but I explained to him that actually we wouldn't be seeing grand-dad any more, which made me sad. He thought about this for a while and then asked, 'When everyone's dead and in heaven, who will drive the cars?'

I often wonder what it will mean for him to have experienced the death of a parent at such a tender age – what Jane Smiley in *A Thousand Acres* describes as a 'misfortune for which there is no compensation'. Will it make him forever aware of the proximity of death in life: anxious, unstable, reckless? Or perhaps he'll be more compassionate and grounded, having learned so early the truths that it takes many of us a lifetime to encounter. A shockingly high proportion of young offenders in prison have lost someone close to them at a tender age; on the other hand, I heard a radio programme which claimed that losing a parent young can be a spur to success in later life. It could go either way.

I thought hard about my own role in Ruairi's life. I had been trying to be both banks of the river – mother and father – but it's hard enough to be one parent, let alone two. (I once remarked to Ruairi that, if you crossed 'Daddy' and 'Mummy', you got my name – 'Maddy'. With typical wit, he thought for a moment and replied, 'Or "Dummy".') I would surely need a lot of strength to stand up to my growing boy, but I am not a man, and the effort was exhausting me. I vowed instead to be the best mother I could – the moon rather than the sun – and let him find others to take on some of the fathering role.

My stay at Park Attwood had helped to restore my spirit, but my body was still in crisis. The patches of lost hair were slowly starting to grow back in little wisps of white, but I had absolutely no energy and my legs felt weak and trembling much of the time. I consulted a gastro-enterologist about the perpetual tight feeling like a knot in my stomach, and was referred for an endoscopy, where a fibre-optic camera is inserted down your throat to view the inside of your stomach. This procedure was far worse than I'd imagined – I'd opted to have it without sedation – and I panicked and gagged as the tube passed down my throat. A kind male nurse held on to my hand throughout, reminding me to keep breathing. The test showed a small stomach ulcer; I would need to take medication, and then have a repeat endoscopy to check that it had gone. I got myself home, seriously shaken, and wept for the fact that there was no one there to ask how it had gone, to make me a cup of tea and put their arms around me.

Everyone seemed relieved that something concrete had been diagnosed, and of course told me that ulcers can be caused by stress (in fact the majority are from bacterial infection). I was glad that something specific had been found, that after months of inconclusive tests I was diagnosed as properly 'ill'; however, I didn't believe that the ulcer was the reason for my illness, but just one of its manifestations. I spent Christmas on a medication that seemed to shut down my stomach completely, making it almost impossible to eat, and I returned to the hospital in January for the second test, which gave me the all-clear.

I have seen from my sister's long journey with Chronic Fatigue Syndrome how the symptoms come and go, changing over time so that they seem to indicate first one condition then another. This kind of total breakdown of the body is mysterious and defies accurate measure; the diagnosis of CFS seems to be *faute de mieux*: a cluster of amorphous, shifting pains and problems which can render some people bed-bound and unable even to speak, whilst others live the lives of the walking wounded. Meanwhile blood tests and the like reveal nothing abnormal. No wonder it is hard for those who haven't experienced it to quite believe in it – not unlike grief.

To her credit my doctor had not offered me anti-depressants – often an easy resort for the undiagnosable – although several friends urged me to give them a try. I was pretty certain that depression was not the cause of my symptoms, even if living with them day after day had brought me very low. Of course, I knew it was somehow precipitated by the shock of Michael's sudden death – how could it not be? That was a major part of my story, of who I was. But the manifestations of it were strikingly physical, and I didn't feel that mucking around with my brain chemistry would necessarily improve matters.

I had kept on with my painting class, though it was an exhausting endeavour to get myself and all my equipment over to Hampstead every week. But I sensed that the work I did there was an important part of my recovery. I had done a series of paintings of myself and Michael, at first young and in love, and then separated by death; one of them showed the dream I had had the day before he died, where he told me it was time for him to go. Now I moved on to exploring themes from fairy-tales and myths, which have always gripped me with their archetypal resonance – Bluebeard, the Snow Queen, the Handless Maiden. It was as if I were searching for keys to unlock the darkest chambers of my mind, to find out where the bodies were buried. Paintings have a kind of secret emotional language, which you can't explain in words. At the time of making them, I often can't say what the paintings are about, but I often find that they 'foretell' emotional changes, sometimes by a year or more; in this way they are not so much directly therapeutic, but work rather like dreams, to reveal the direction one must go in.

And what of Michael? Three years may seem a long time, but in terms of mourning it was just a start, barely enough time to get used to the practicalities of living without him. He wasn't in my head at every moment, as he had been for the first year, nor absent and hard to conjure, as he had been in the second. He seemed to have settled into being a constant point of reference – many times a day, something would remind me and I'd stop and think of him, consider what he might have thought about a situation, or feel a desperate pang of loss. Or something would strike me as funny, and I'd realise that I was looking forward to sharing the joke with him.

People talk in terms of 'getting over' grief, 'moving on', and recently that dreadful word 'closure', but I doubt you ever leave it behind. Loss is loss, and the pain of it is forever intense, although over time it comes less often and is perhaps less overwhelming. It's more that you become accustomed to grief; it becomes a part of who you are, like a scarred but still sensitive wound. It was as if I had got used to missing Michael, but I still felt as if I were in limbo, waiting for my life to start again.

One thing that kept me connected to Michael was my involvement in his work. The young man had been continuing to catalogue the books, and he and I had begun to collect Michael's prose writings for an anthology, which would be published as a companion volume to the *Collected Poems* the following year. This I found an immensely enjoyable process that stretched my brain in ways that I had forgotten and gave me a further insight into the brilliance and originality of Michael's mind. I felt more in touch with his intellectual life now than I had when he was alive, when my role had been more one of a practical and emotional support. He was also such a funny writer, and it felt good to laugh in his memory instead of cry.

In January my mother was taken into hospital after collapsing in the middle of the night, and, although they couldn't find anything specific wrong with her, it was clear that she could no longer live alone. She moved into a care home for two months, and we rather hoped she would stay there, since there was no question of her living with either me or my sister. But she was so unhappy and kicked up such a fuss, frequently threatening to kill herself, that we had to arrange a live-in carer so that she could go home. Gradually we were realising that her confusion was more than just old age; at her eightieth birthday party she clearly didn't recognise many of the guests, all family. Dementia creeps up subtly and is initially well concealed; there is a relatively brief window when a person is aware they are becoming confused and makes huge efforts to cover it up, then the fog descends.

My sister had taken the lion's share of looking after her: running around to do shopping, sort out her medicine and deal with daily crises. She has always had a very different relationship with my mother from mine; although in many ways I am more like my mother, I think my sister has always been the favourite. I can say this now without rancour, although it caused me considerable pain over the years, particularly once my father died and I realised I had lost an advocate. It is strange how you can grow up in the same family but with such different experiences. As the first child, apart from the usual role – the induction of novice parents – I also took the brunt of my mother's mental illness, to some extent shielding my sister. Of course we both suffered from the lack of proper mothering, but, whereas I was pitched into insecurity and melancholy, my sister took on the role of carer and cheerer-upper. 'She was such a kind child!' my mother always said to me – in which I could not help but hear the sub-text: 'And you weren't.'

I only have one child, so I don't know what it is like to feel that you connect more strongly, or perhaps more straightforwardly, with one child than with another. I've always felt a very strong bond with Ruairi, a kind of deep recognition, even though he is very different from me in many ways. In those early weeks, when I held my longed-for baby in my arms, I sometimes thought my heart would burst with joy, and, on his first birthday, I joked that I wanted to buy him a pedestal, such was my worship of him.

It helps that Ruairi is a boy, and therefore in a sense completely 'other'. I have no fear (as Michael did) that he will somehow turn into me as he grows up, and I am secure that my relationship with him will be different from mine with my mother. I heard a radio programme about a man who gave his wife a kidney, and it set me thinking whether I would have done the same for Michael. I was shocked to find that the decision was by no means automatic, although I imagine I would have come round to it in the end. What was clear to me, though, is that I would give Ruairi both my kidneys in a heartbeat.

When I was born, a very large baby and three weeks late, my mother was totally unprepared for the reality of labour, which she went through in a state of terror and shock, hallucinating from the gas and air. After I was born, she refused to see me for the first twenty-four hours, convinced that there was something horribly wrong with me. Even when my father assured her that I was the most beautiful baby in the ward (I had long curly dark hair and baby-doll blue eyes), she could not bring herself to believe it. I think I must have represented the bringing to birth of all her fears and self-doubts, the sense of inner wrongness she carried and which she has passed on to me. I recently found out from her medical records that she was depressed during pregnancy, and I strongly suspect post-natally, though I doubt that this was recognised or that any help was forthcoming.

Perhaps this kind of traumatic beginning on earth can be compensated for if everything goes smoothly thereafter: mother and baby bonding, mother growing in confidence as a parent. But my mother seemed to take pleasure in telling me throughout my childhood that my birth had been 'the worst day of her life'. Michael had also been separated from his mother at birth, because she suffered congestive heart failure. I sometimes wonder if that lonely beginning was one of the deep links that bound us; a friend of his once commented that we shared 'the same inner sadness'. But in his childhood Michael was clearly his mother's favourite, an angelically well-behaved child who clung tightly to her hand. He must have made his older sister sick.

In March I had a session with my therapist that from one day to the next seemed to turn my health around. I can't explain what happened exactly, but I got very angry about something and, rather than back away from it, my therapist encouraged me to feel it fully. As I left the room I could feel the start of a feverish cold, the kind of 'proper' illness I had not been well enough to get for over a year. I knew immediately that this was a strong illness which would make my immune system stand up and fight; I could feel strength returning, even as I lay in bed coughing and sneezing.

Like my mother, I often turn anger on myself rather than express it properly, which leads to misery and self-hatred, a pattern learned very early on in childhood. My mother was in an almost constant state of suppressed fury, but she would rarely admit to feeling angry. However, we knew the signs – the twitching shoulder, the set mouth and too-bright voice – and learned to keep our heads down. If we argued with her, she just cut us dead, and we had to grovel and apologise, whereupon she pretended that nothing had happened. In fact I was a very emotional child; I raged and howled and sobbed, finding small disappointments and setbacks almost unbearable, but as my mother had no idea how to contain her own feelings, she certainly couldn't contain mine for me.

In the early days of my relationship with Michael, I was emotionally volatile; I had to storm off in a rage several times in order to assure myself that he would come after me and still love me despite my extremes of feeling. Michael also struggled to express anger outwardly, as in his family it had frequently led to physical violence. He once kicked a brick wall in frustration, badly bruising a toe; at other times, unable to express what he was feeling, he would withdraw into a sort of psychotic state where I could not reach him. What a damaged pair we were!

At Easter Ruairi and I spent a week in Cornwall in a cottage by the sea owned by the Sand Rose Trust, a charity which gives free holidays to bereaved families. It was in a glorious position overlooking St Michael's Mount, with beautiful gardens and a room for quiet contemplation. The weather was warm enough to go to the beach, where Ruairi would hurl himself into the icy sea, and we took gentle strolls along the cliffs. I was beginning to feel a lot better, although I could still only manage to walk short distances.

One morning at the cottage I woke up and suddenly felt more 'normal', as if I was coming back to life. It was as though I had walked through a doorway from one section of the journey into another; I pictured a series of secret courtyard gardens, connected by circular oriental gateways. I felt much lighter, as if I had at last put down some of the heavy burden I had been carrying. Helped by the sea air and exercise, my health was improving day by day, and when we got back to London I found I had the energy to do things that even a month before would have been unthinkable.

Since it was clear we were no longer going to move, I decided to make changes at home, starting with the large front room, which had been Michael's study – perhaps the best room in the house. I had used it for the computer and to store my painting equipment, but it remained much as it was when Michael died, cluttered with his books and papers. With the help of my young co-editor, we stacked seventy-five boxes of these up in the loft; then I hired builders to turn it into a smart new grown-up living-room. The value of a new space is that you can decide exactly what to put into it, rather like a new life. I took the opportunity to sort ruthlessly through my own stuff, disposing of many of the books I had been dragging around with me over the years.

I didn't know what to do with Michael's large record collection. The records had not been played for years, since the record-player's stylus mysteriously disappeared when Ruairi was a toddler, but parting with them was more painful than I had expected: not just the music, which had of course been the theme tunes of our life together, but the records themselves in their covers, which were almost as meaningful. I distributed the large number of Irish music records among our musician friends, and took the rest to Oxfam, photographing all the covers before letting them go. For a while I was in mourning for them, wondering if I'd done the right thing.

Our old upstairs living-room became a big new teenage bedroom for Ruairi; he disposed ruthlessly of all his old childhood toys, except for a few cherished cuddlies, which he buried deep in the cupboard. His bedroom became a study and, I hoped, a room to paint in – I had used it as a studio when we first moved in, before Ruairi was born. In a matter of months we had drastically reshaped our living space, and shed many possessions. It had been an exhausting process both physically and emotionally, but at last I felt I was taking charge of my future.

That summer I reached fifty, the age at which Michael had died; it felt very strange to be overtaking him. To celebrate my birthday, I held an exhibition of my paintings at Ruairi's school, which was in a beautiful converted Victorian church. I felt very proud as I looked at all the work I had produced in the past four years, hung on the walls of the nave. Although I paint principally for myself, art is a form of communication, and to share it with others was thrilling. At the party that night I performed some songs with my sister and another friend, including one of Michael's poems which I had set to music.

In August I spent a week in Switzerland at the Alexander Technique International Congress, which is held every four years – the last one had been just before Michael's death

– then took a bus over the mountain pass to Lake Como in Italy. Michael and I had been on a day-trip there from Milan twenty years before, and it stands out in my mind as one of those unexpectedly perfect days that you simply can't plan for. We had explored winding goat paths through the hills, come across a perfect tiny town with a waterfall running through it, then taken a boat back along the lake in the golden evening light. There was something of the pilgrimage in my revisiting this spot, a need to touch again the feeling of that special time with Michael, and I was not disappointed. Italy is an unashamedly beautiful and romantic place, and my few days there filled my heart and bathed me in sunshine.

One afternoon, sitting on a rock in the beating sun after a swim in the cold lake, I became acutely aware of the feeling of the cool, rough stone against my hand and the balmy air on my skin. I felt perfectly content, perfectly present, and asked myself why life couldn't feel like that all of the time. I have flashes like this every so often – I think of them as 'moments of grace' – which descend unbidden and evaporate quickly when I try to hold on to them. They give me the clear sense that everything is exactly as it should be, which of course is not unlike how I felt during the days of Michael's death.

'Our Life Stories' . . .

The last two years of Michael's life, despite our marriage and his new-found happiness as a father, were fraught with anxieties about both his health and his career. Perhaps it was something of a mid-life crisis as he headed towards fifty. He'd had recurrent, although not life-threatening, heart problems – palpitations and misfired beats – for a few years, which terrified him and made him more conscious than ever of his mortality. This may well have been behind his change of heart which led to our marriage. He went running regularly and made an effort to eat wisely, but found it almost impossible to keep a lid on stress.

After the trip to America, during which he was seriously ill with a blocked bile duct, he was scheduled to have his gall bladder removed a few days after his fiftieth birthday. We tried to celebrate the day by seeing a film together and going for a meal, but he felt so unwell that it wasn't much fun. The gall-bladder operation should have left him feeling a lot better, but things didn't seem to improve much and he continued having digestive problems and a general feeling of malaise.

He had also got into a state of extreme stress over the state of British poetry, which he saw as under siege from a particular group of academically-based writers who disliked him and his colleagues – the poets who published books that people actually wanted to read. I'm not sure how much of this was real, and how much in his mind, but he became quite paranoid at times about the supposed takeover of the poetry establishment by this faction. Perhaps he sensed that time was running out and wanted to make sure his reputation was safe for posterity. Never one to engage in open conflict, he spent hours writing blogs and reviews under pseudonyms, and composing a series of perfectly credible spoof avant-garde poems to prove a point.

A real blow came when Oxford University Press, his former publisher, which had abandoned its poetry list a few years previously, *forcing him to move to Picador, brought out a major anthology of British and Irish poetry in which he was not included. He was not by any means the only contemporary poet left out, but he took it very personally, because he had known the editor in Chicago. In fact Michael's reputation as a writer has continued to grow, prompted in no small measure by his untimely death. As Jimi Hendrix put it: 'Once you're dead, you're made for life!'*

Our last year together was overshadowed by all of this, and I often had the sense that he was slipping away from me into his own preoccupations and anxieties. I had enjoyed our wedding, and the honeymoon had been very romantic. But I can't say that I much liked being married – I felt slightly trapped, and had the uncomfortable feeling that I'd signed up for the long haul as we declined into old age. I had visions of myself changing incontinence pads and spoon-feeding him, a grumpy old man. Probably deep inside I still cherished a fantasy that marriage would transform him, change the balance of our relationship so that I felt more supported, but of course things stayed resolutely the same. I was wrong about the long haul, though.

Our lives took on a slightly frantic quality again, with me absorbed in finishing my course, juggling that with parenthood, and Michael nursing his obsessions and ill health. He had at last begun to acknowledge that his stress levels were unsustainable and sought help; he'd been waiting over a year for an appointment with the local mental health services, which with typical irony finally came through the week of his death.

If I'm honest I couldn't say when we last had a truly happy or relaxed time in each other's company, although superficially life went on as normal, and Ruairi – our 'little angel of cheerfulness', as we called him – kept us grounded in the here and now. This probably explains why my first reaction to Michael's death was a sense of relief that I no longer had to look after him. It has taken all the years since then to really comprehend what he meant to me, what his death has taken from me; this infuriating, adorable, complex, talented, troubled, loving soul-mate. 'An amazing man inside a very strange one', as a friend put it at the memorial.

Chapter 11

Grief was no longer such a sharp pain – more of a melancholy edge to life, like the crinkled black borders of the Catholic mass card Michael's cousin sent from America on the anniversary of his death. Events this year would make heavy demands on me, what Michael would have called 'one thing during another'. The quest to build a new life for myself was put on the back burner while I was swept up in the needs and dramas of those close to me: my mother, who finally had to be moved into a nursing home so that we could continue to pay for her care by selling her house; and Ruairi, as he eventually left the Steiner school where he had been since the age of one, with its community of old friends and support networks. Both of these were painful endings.

Michael's two posthumous books were to be published and the South Bank Centre hosted a launch event on St Patrick's Day: a whole afternoon's programme, including a panel discussion, a reception with an Irish band, followed by the performance of a suite of seven pieces for 'prepared' piano by the composer Terry Mann, which he had dedicated to Michael and which included recordings of him reading the poems. Although I had been involved in planning the event, the pressure of other problems meant that I rather took my eye off the ball, and two weeks before the launch few tickets had been sold, and many people told me they had not heard about it. I drafted in everyone I could think of to circulate publicity and managed to drum up a reasonable crowd at the last minute.

Many of the audience had known Michael personally, so there was a strong sense of memorialising the man alongside celebrating the work; which was also true of newspaper reviews of the book, which were full of personal anecdotes. I think it might take a generation for Michael's charming personality to get out of the way of his impact as a writer. But we had done what we could – the books would have to find their own way from now on. On the way home, I said to Ruairi, 'Let's put Daddy back in the box now, shall we?'

In need of a break, I booked a week at a retreat centre in southern Spain, choosing almost at random a course called 'Family Constellations Therapy', which sounded interesting. It was strange going back to Spain, where I had last been the week before Michael died. I had thought then that I would never return, but there seemed something symbolic about this journey – I hoped it might be a kind of 'bookend' to a painful period of my life.

Family Constellations Therapy is hard to explain except by experiencing it. You choose people from the group to represent members of your family and simply place them in relation to each other in the centre of the room – a 'constellation', which can even include people who have died. Those chosen to be representatives in the constellation then say what the dynamic feels like to them, not just emotionally but bodily, and are encouraged to move position if they wish. How this comes about I am at a loss to say, except that it works in a very physical way; your body tells you what to do. Even if you are not chosen to participate, it is fascinating to watch, like a really good play.

When it came to my turn, my 'constellation' threw up an interesting new dynamic around my grandfather, my mother's father. It seemed to show that his First World War service in the Ambulance Corps – two years scraping up bodies from the battlefields of northern France – might be at the root of some of my mother's distress. Emotional patterns that are not fully dealt with frequently get passed on from generation to generation – 'It deepens like a coastal shelf', as Larkin put it. Like many ex-soldiers, my grandfather never spoke of his traumatic experience of war, but it was clearly difficult for him to connect emotionally with his own children: they were all devoted to him, but terrified of his emotional volatility. My mother, possibly the most sensitive of his four daughters, spent her life trying to get close to him and win his approval; with this desperately unfulfilled relationship taking up all her emotional energy, perhaps she had little left for us.

The group leader, a very experienced therapist, told me she thought I needed to reconnect with my mother; that the troubled bond with her was at the root of much of my sadness and struggle. I knew this, of course, and had spent many years exploring it in psychotherapy, but it was still an open wound in my heart. It often seemed like a hurt I would have to live with and accept for ever – something so deep and fundamental that there was no chance of it ever healing.

She suggested I reach out to the woman I had chosen to represent my mother in the constellation, and suddenly I found myself sobbing loudly in front of the whole group; the process was stronger than I was and it took me over. My 'mother' took me into her arms and held me, and it was as though at last I was getting what I had so long desired, what my own mother would surely have wanted to give me had she been able. Afterwards I felt exhausted but lighter, as if a very heavy weight had been lifted off me. Being able to openly express all that pain in front of witnesses seemed to have released me from its clutches, and deep inside I felt a new sense of calm.

At last I could forgive my mother her inadequacy as a parent, and be grateful for what she did give me – the gift of life. When I next visited her in the nursing home, I thanked her for being my mother. 'Well, I'm not much use to you like this,' she commented. 'But you've always loved me,' I said, to which she replied, 'Yes I have.' It doesn't sound much, but for us it was huge, and after that our relationship became a very simple one, of love. I no longer felt any blame for my mother's failure to love me enough as a child, because I understood that it wasn't really about me. For fifty years I had carried a sense of somehow not being good enough whatever I did, of being innately unloveable. Even the great embracing, forgiving, warm love of Michael for twenty-one of those years had not healed this wound, and it was no surprise that the sudden shocking loss of him had ripped it open again.

As the week in Spain drew to a close, I began to realise that I had also put down a large part of my grieving for Michael. On the final day there I had the opportunity to do another 'constellation', this time choosing a representative for Michael. I experienced very strongly once more what an incredible bond of love there had been between us, and how hard it was to bring that to an end; when we said goodbye to each other and let go, I once again wept openly.

It is no coincidence that at the same time as the emotional umbilical cord with my mother was re-established, the one with my dead husband could finally be cut. Only now that I was more firmly attached to life could I at last acknowledge that he is gone. He will always be a huge part of me, of course, as well as living on through his son, and I will always mourn his loss and miss him. Most of all, I miss the jokes and the hugs. But now I am able to think of him with less of an overwhelming sense of sadness, and more of a sweet regret.

Above all, I am filled with gratitude for the enormous and unconditional gift of love that he gave me.

POSTSCRIPT

If this were a novel it would end with a new romance: the beginning of a new story. But life is more complex: as one strand concludes, others are still threading onward – a continuing dance between the inner self and the outer path we have to tread. Sometimes all that has happened is that the light in the room has changed, in a subtle but very profound way.

I have become 'acquainted with death', and through it I've become better acquainted with life – its fragility and its strength. More, I've come to acknowledge the strength within its fragility, like a tree that bends in the storm but doesn't snap. A friend who worked as a photographer in Sudan during a terrible famine told me how, in the midst of such overwhelming suffering and disaster, she witnessed the amazing will of the human spirit to survive, to live, to laugh even. Everything contains its opposite – death is in the centre of life, life in the centre of death. I've learned that you do not leave grief and loss behind you, rather you incorporate them into your being and let them enrich and deepen you and your understanding of what really matters.

As the tellers of the old tales knew, you can make a journey to the underworld and return. Sometimes you can even bring back gifts; but in exchange you usually have to leave behind something or someone very precious to you. It's the bargain we make for this incredible privilege of life.

I paused at the curtain, looked back once, left.

ACKNOWLEDGEMENTS

For their support, help, encouragement and belief in this book I would like to thank Maura Dooley, Rosalind Paxman, Jennifer Hewson, Arash Hejazi and Sam Barden.

Michael Donaghy's *Collected Poems* is published by Picador, 2009.

ABOUT THE TITLE

In Sumerian legend, the goddess Inanna, Queen of Heaven, descends into the earth to console her furious widowed sister, Ereshkigal, Queen of the Underworld. At each of seven doorways, she is stripped of one of her royal garments and powers, until she is hung on a hook naked and left for dead. The water god, Enki, sends two creatures deep into the earth to rescue her; they appease Ereshkigal by sympathizing with her troubles, and she allows Inanna to be restored to life and return to the world above.